GOOD HOUSEKEEPING

Successful

MICROWAVE

BAKING

GOOD HOUSEKEEPING

Successful

MICROWAVE

BAKING

EBURY PRESS, LONDON

Published by Ebury Press
Division of The National Magazine Company Limited
Colquhoun House
27-37 Broadwick Street
London W1V 1FR

First Impression 1987

ISBN 0 85223 680 8 (Hardback)
0 85223 685 9 (Paperback)

Senior Editor: *Fiona MacIntyre*
Editor: *Felicity Jackson*
Designer: *Grahame Dudley*
Photography: *James Murphy*
Stylist: *Cathy Sinker*
Cookery: *Janet Smith* and *Susanna Tee*
Illustrations: *Dennis Curran*

Filmset by Advanced Filmsetters (Glasgow) Limited
Printed in Great Britain at the University Press, Cambridge

CONTENTS

INTRODUCTION

Feather-light cakes rise before your eyes as if by magic when they are cooked in the microwave. Breads and biscuits are equally successful, and all cook in a fraction of the time it takes in a conventional oven.

The very fast, moist cooking does mean, however, that they do not develop their characteristic crisp, brown surface and they can look quite unappealing unless given a touch of colour. There are various ways of doing this, either before or after cooking.

Ingredients such as wholemeal flour, cocoa powder, brown sugar, treacle, nuts, sesame seeds and fruits can be added to the cake mixture. Pale cakes will look more golden if they have orange or lemon rind and juice added to them. Alternatively, the cooked cake can be iced, decorated, or covered with whipped cream to make it look more attractive.

Breads, too, can be made with wholemeal flour, which gives them a good colour. They do not have the crisp outer crust of conventionally baked bread because moisture is drawn to the surface of the bread during microwaving, but they can be finished off under a hot grill to crisp and brown the surface.

Shortcrust pastry can also be made with wholemeal flour, and if the pastry is rolled out very thinly it is possible to achieve a crisp result. Even pale flan cases look attractive once a filling is added. Filled pies reheated in the microwave will not be crisp because of the steam produced by the filling.

It is possible to cook puff pastry and achieve a crispy, flaky result by following the instructions on page 54. The pastry will not brown, but can be decorated with icing to add colour.

Some crisp biscuits cannot be cooked in the microwave, but there are many others that cook extremely well. The stickier types, such as flapjacks, which are cooked in one piece and then cut into squares or bars are ideal. They need to be watched carefully, however, as any food with a high sugar content reaches a very high temperature much more quickly than other foods and may burn in the centre or in patches, even though the surface may look uncooked.

The microwave is perfect for small quantities of biscuits, particularly as there is no need to preheat the oven, but for larger batches, a conventional oven may be easier as it can accommodate more biscuits per batch.

EQUIPMENT

The choice of container for baking is important, and a wide variety is now available. For cakes, a round, shallow container, such as a microware cake dish, is best. Cakes will cook faster and more thoroughly in shallow containers than in deep ones—if the mixture is too deep and in a large container, the centre of the cake will not cook. Ring moulds are also ideal and ensure even, overall cooking. It is possible to improvise a ring mould by placing a heavy glass tumbler in the centre of a round dish, then pouring the mixture around it.

Cakes cooked in a loaf dish will tend to cook at the ends before the centre is ready, so care must be taken to avoid overcooking, and some mixtures are best cooked on MEDIUM power (see individual recipes).

Cook small cakes in paper cases (using two per cake for extra support) and stand them in a microwave muffin tray, ramekins or cups to support the paper cases during cooking.

It is important to use the container size specified in the recipe, but if this is not possible, remember that if a larger container is used, the cake will cook in less time because a greater surface area is exposed to the microwaves. If using smaller containers than those specified, they must not be overfilled. Cake containers should not be more than half-full, otherwise the cake—which will rise higher than a conventionally cooked one—may spill over the top whilst in the microwave.

Specialised microwave cooking containers include muffin trays or bun trays which can be used for muffins, small cakes or individual pastry tarts; baking trays for biscuits; browning dishes, skillets and griddles which can be used to cook scones as well as savoury dishes.

The containers used for the recipes in this book are as follows:
   shallow 23 cm (9 inch) square dish
   20.5 cm (8 inch) round cake dish with a loose bottom
   shallow 18 × 23 cm (7 × 9 inch) dish
   shallow 12.5 × 23 cm (5 × 9 inch) dish
   25.5 cm (10 inch) round dish
   1.7 litre (3 pint) loaf dish measuring 12.5 × 20.5 × 7.5 cm
      (5 × 8 × 3 inches)
   1.6 litre (2¾ pint) ring mould measuring 21.5 cm (8½ inches) in diameter
   1.1 litre (2 pint) ring mould measuring 23 cm (9 inches) in diameter
   deep 20.5 cm (8 inch) round dish
   7.5 × 11 cm (3 × 4½ inch) 350 ml (12 fl oz) dish

The bowl sizes used are:
SMALL, about 900 ml (1½ pints)
MEDIUM, about 2.3 litres (4 pints)
LARGE, about 3.4 litres (6 pints)

PREPARING CONTAINERS

Cakes cooked in the microwave tend to be more fragile than conventionally baked cakes and are, therefore, more likely to break when turned out if they stick slightly in the container.

Be guided by conventional rules about greasing and lining containers for either cakes, bread or biscuits, but avoid flouring dishes as this produces an unpalatable coating on the cake. Cakes baked in a plastic container will not need greasing unless the mixture contains only a small amount of fat, but other containers should be greased and the base of larger containers lined with greaseproof paper.

COOKING TECHNIQUES

Most of the cake recipes in this book use the all-in-one method which is wonderfully quick and easy to prepare and is ideal for microwave cooking. All the ingredients are simply beaten together with a wooden spoon for 2–3 minutes until well blended and slightly glossy. An electric mixer can be used, but take care not to overbeat.

The all-in-one method uses soft tub margarine, block margarine or softened butter (see Quick Tips for softening butter). Mixtures should be of a softer consistency than when baked conventionally to ensure a good, even rise and moist result. If you want to adapt one of your own conventional recipes for the microwave, follow the nearest microwave equivalent for timings and add an extra 15–30 ml (1–2 tbsp) milk for each egg used in the mixture.

ARRANGING

Most cakes benefit from being cooked on a roasting rack as this enables maximum penetration of the microwaves and ensures that the cake is cooked in the centre. This will not be necessary if your cooker has a shelf. (If you do not have a roasting rack, use an upturned soup bowl instead.) It is not necessary with small cakes.

When cooking a number of small cakes or biscuits, arrange them in a circle, about 5 cm (2 inches) apart. Do not put one in the middle. If it is not possible to place them in a circle, rearrange the items during cooking, placing the outer items towards the centre and vice versa.

COVERING

Covering food during cooking keeps it moist, but cakes that are covered will be similar in texture to a sponge pudding. Baked foods such as breads, teabreads and pastries are not covered because they do not require moist cooking. In the recipes in this book food is uncovered unless otherwise stated.

When a recipe specifies covering, cover the container *completely* either with a lid or an inverted plate. At the time of going to press, it has been recommended by the Ministry of Agriculture, Fisheries and Food that cling film should not be used in microwave cooking, as it has been found that some of the plasticiser di-2-ethyhexledipate (DEHA) used to soften cling film can migrate into the food during cooking.

TURNING

In all forms of cooking it is important to make sure the food cooks evenly, and the best way to do this is to turn and stir the food. Solid foods, such as cakes, cannot be stirred so the container needs to be turned. Even if your cooker has a turntable, it is a good idea to change the position of the food by giving the container a half or quarter turn once or twice during the cooking time to ensure an even result. This is particularly important if you find that cakes rise unevenly, or if your cooker has hot or cold spots where food cooks at a faster or slower rate than elsewhere in the cooker.

COOKING

Always undercook cakes rather than overcook, they can be returned to the cooker for a few extra minutes if necessary, but overcooked cakes will be dry and this cannot be rectified.

Various factors affect the cooking times, such as whether the ingredients are warm or cold, or whether you have just used the cooker and the floor is still warm. If you turn out a cake and find that it is uncooked at the bottom, simply invert it on to a plate and return it to the cooker on the plate and cook for a further 1–3 minutes. Some cakes may have a small circle of mixture on the base which looks less cooked than the rest of the cake, but as long as it is not raw there is no need to worry about this.

TESTING FOR DONENESS

Some cakes are tested by inserting a skewer or wooden cocktail stick into the centre – the cake is done when it comes out clean; other cakes should be removed from the cooker while still moist in areas on the surface (normally they would be considered slightly underdone). It varies according to the type of mixture and whether the dish is covered, so follow the instructions in the individual recipes.

Breads, teabreads and biscuits, which are firmer mixtures, should look dry on the surface.

STANDING TIME

After cooking, the cake should be removed from the cooker and left to stand for 5–15 minutes, depending on the size and density. During this time the heat will equalise throughout the food, and the cooking will be completed by this residual heat. The standing time must always be taken into account when estimating the cooking time of baked goods.

TURNING OUT

Turn out the cake after it has been left to stand, and immediately peel away the paper to prevent it sticking. Fragile soft cakes should be turned out on to a tea-towel placed over a wire rack to prevent the rack cutting into the cake.

COMBINED COOKERS

Combined cookers combine conventional and microwave methods of cooking so that food browns as well as cooks quickly. One of the disadvantages of cooking in a microwave cooker is that baked goods do not brown or crisp. This book shows you how to overcome these disadvantages, but if you own a combined cooker, follow your manufacturer's instructions on the technique of browning or crisping a dish.

FACTORS THAT AFFECT COOKING

There are various factors, such as the density, composition and starting temperature of the food, that affect the cooking time when baking in the microwave.

DENSITY

Microwaves can penetrate light, porous foods more quickly than dense ones, so cakes and biscuits cook much faster than joints of meat.

TEMPERATURE OF FOOD

Food microwaved straight from the refrigerator will take longer than food at room temperature. In the recipes in this book, food is at room temperature unless otherwise specified.

QUICK TIPS

■ To soften butter, place in a bowl and microwave on LOW for about 1 minute until softened slightly.

■ To melt chocolate, break it into small pieces, unless using chocolate chips, and microwave on LOW just until the chocolate is soft and glossy on top. Remove from the cooker and stir until melted. Block cooking chocolate heats more slowly; as a guide, 100 g (4 oz) cooking chocolate takes about 4 minutes on LOW. The melting times vary according to the material and shape of container used, so it is advisable to check every minute during melting. Take care not to overcook and do not melt on HIGH or the chocolate may scorch.

■ To soften brown sugar which has become hard and lumpy, microwave it on HIGH for 30–50 seconds in the original packaging.

■ If golden syrup or honey has crystallised, the texture can be restored by microwaving on HIGH for 1–2 minutes. Remove metal lids and only do this to products in glass jars, otherwise transfer to an ovenproof bowl. Do not microwave for longer than specified as the glass is not heatproof.

■ To remove the skins and brown hazelnuts, place them on a single layer of absorbent kitchen paper and microwave on HIGH for 30 seconds. Rub off the skins, then place them on a large plate and microwave on HIGH until just golden, stirring frequently.

■ To toast 25–100 g (1–4 oz) flaked almonds, place them on a large plate and microwave on HIGH for 8–10 minutes, stirring frequently, until golden brown.

■ Blanch almonds by covering 100 g (4 oz) nuts with 150 ml ($\frac{1}{4}$ pint) water. Microwave on HIGH for about 2 minutes. Drain and slip the skins off with your fingers.

■ Lemons and other citrus fruit will yield more juice if microwaved on HIGH for 30 seconds before squeezing.

■ To plump sultanas or raisins, cover with water and microwave on HIGH for 5 minutes. Stir, leave to stand, then drain and dry with absorbent kitchen paper before using.

■ Save time when making bread by speeding up the rising process with the help of your microwave. Put the dough in a large bowl, cover with a clean tea-towel and microwave on HIGH for 15 seconds, then leave it to stand for 5 minutes. Repeat the microwaving and standing five or six times until the dough springs back when pressed lightly with the fingertips.

PROBLEM-SOLVER

I f you read the introduction and then follow the recipes carefully, using the exact amounts of ingredients and the correct size dishes, you should achieve perfect results every time. If, however, your cake, teabread or pastry is not successful or if you have tried unsuccessfully to convert your favourite conventional recipe then here are some tips to help you discover what went wrong.

Uncooked circle of mixture on base of cake or teabread
■ The bottom of a deep cake or teabread cooks most slowly. Cook standing on a roasting rack or upturned plate. Return partly uncooked cakes to the oven inverted on to a plate and cook for 1–3 minutes on HIGH. Be careful not to overcook you should remove the mixture as soon as it has set. A dark circle of mixture will still be visible after extra cooking but will not show once the cake is filled and decorated.
■ Oven setting incorrect (see page 12).

One large patch of a cake or teabread burned
■ Oven has a hotspot. Turn cakes frequently during cooking.

Burned patches throughout a cake or teabread

Lumpy sugar added to the mixture. The lumps of sugar get very hot during cooking and result in burned patches.

Too much dried fruit added. Dried fruit contains a high proportion of sugar and has the same effect as lumps of sugar. If using your own recipe, cut down on the amount of fruit. Alternatively, try washing the fruit before coating it in flour. This should cut down on very sticky surfaces.

Too much sugar in the cake mixture. If adapting your own cake or teabread recipe it may be unsuitable.

Cake or teabread is dry

Not enough liquid added. Mixtures should be more moist than conventional cakes; add an extra 15–30 ml (1–2 tbsp) milk for every egg.

Cooking time too long. See notes in introduction on testing when a cake or teabread is cooked (page 9).

Mixture should have been covered during cooking. A cover helps retain moisture, see notes on covering in the introduction (page 8).

Bread very dry

Mixture too dry, add more liquid.

Cooking time too long. See notes in introduction (page 9) on testing when bread is cooked.

Teabread dry at ends but moist in centre

Cooking time too long. Watch teabreads during cooking: the ends will cook much faster than the centre. When the centre rises, test to see if cooked.

Power level incorrect. Some teabreads benefit from being cooked on a MEDIUM setting.

Dish not turned during cooking. If the teabread is rising unevenly, it means that it is cooking unevenly. Watch during cooking and turn if necessary.

One biscuit burns, others don't

Oven has a hotspot. When cooking next batch of biscuits arrange in a circle, leaving a space where biscuit burned previously.

Biscuits very chewy

Cooking time too short. Increase cooking time by 30 seconds, test one biscuit then repeat if necessary.

Mixture not suitable for cooking in a microwave.

Oven setting incorrect (see page 12).

Biscuit tough

Cooking time too long. Decrease cooking time by about 1 minute.

Mixture not suitable for cooking in a microwave.

Pastry soggy

Pastry rolled out too thickly.

Cooking time too short. Increase cooking time by 30 seconds–1 minute, test again and repeat if necessary.

Pastry case loses shape during cooking

Pastry not pricked sufficiently before cooking.

Pastry rolled out too thickly.

Flaky pastry burns

Amount of pastry too large to cook in the microwave. See recipe for cream slices for ideal size of pastry (page 54).

Flaky pastry soggy and does not rise

Pastry rolled out too thickly.

Recipe and method not suitable for cooking in the microwave.

HOW TO USE THE RECIPES IN THIS BOOK WITH YOUR COOKER SETTINGS

Unlike conventional ovens, the power output and heat controls on various microwave cookers do not follow a standard formula. When manufacturers refer to a 700-watt cooker, they are referring to the cooker's POWER OUTPUT; its INPUT, which is indicated on the back of the cooker, is double that figure. The higher the wattage of a cooker, the faster the rate of cooking, thus food cooked at 700 watts on full power cooks in half the time of food cooked at 350 watts. That said, the actual cooking performance of one 700-watt cooker may vary slightly from another with the same wattage because factors such as cooker cavity size affect cooking performance. The vast majority of microwave cookers sold today are either 600, 650 or 700 watts, but there are many cookers still in use which may be 400 and 500 watts.

IN THIS BOOK
HIGH refers to 100%/full power output of 600–700 watts.
MEDIUM refers to 60% of full power.
LOW is 35% of full power.

Whatever the wattage of your cooker, the HIGH/FULL setting will always be 100% of the cooker's output. Thus your highest setting will correspond to HIGH.

However, the MEDIUM and LOW settings used in this book may not be equivalent to the MEDIUM and LOW settings marked on your cooker. As these settings vary according to power input, use the following calculation to estimate the correct setting for a 600–700 watt cooker. This simple calculation should be done before you use the recipes for the first time, to ensure successful results. Multiply the percentage power required by the total number of settings on your cooker and divide by 100. To work out what setting MEDIUM and LOW correspond to on your cooker, use the following calculation.

Medium (60%)
= %Power required
× Total Number
of Cooker Settings
÷ 100 = Correct Setting
$$= \frac{60 \times 9}{100} = 5$$

Low (35%)
= %Power required
× Total Number
of Cooker Settings
÷ 100 = Correct Setting
$$= \frac{35 \times 9}{100} = 3$$

If your cooker power output is lower than 600 watts, then you must allow a longer cooking and thawing time for all recipes and charts in this book.

Add approximately 10–15 seconds per minute for a 500 watt cooker, and 15–20 seconds per minute for a 400 watt cooker. No matter what the wattage of your cooker is, you should always check food before the end of cooking time, to ensure that it does not get overcooked. Don't forget to allow for standing time.

FOLLOW EITHER METRIC OR IMPERIAL MEASURES FOR THE RECIPES IN THIS BOOK; THEY ARE NOT INTERCHANGEABLE. SIZE 2 EGGS SHOULD BE USED UNLESS OTHERWISE STATED.

Everyday Cakes

The cakes included here are perfect for family teas throughout the week. Making the most of inexpensive ingredients, most use the all-in-one method of preparation and are ready in next to no time.

▪ Spicy Apple Cake ▪

This very moist cake is equally good served warm as a dessert with custard, cream or yogurt.

Makes 16 Slices

450 g (1 lb) cooking apples, peeled, cored and roughly chopped
225 g (8 oz) plain wholemeal flour
10 ml (2 level tsp) baking powder
5 ml (1 level tsp) ground mixed spice
2.5 ml ($\frac{1}{2}$ level tsp) ground cinnamon

100 g (4 oz) softened butter or soft tub margarine
175 g (6 oz) light soft brown sugar
2 eggs
75 ml (5 tbsp) milk
30 ml (2 level tbsp) icing sugar

▪

GREASE a 1.6 litre ($2\frac{3}{4}$ pint) ring mould and scatter a third of the apple in the base.

▪

PUT the flour, baking powder, spices, butter or margarine, sugar, eggs and milk into a bowl and beat until smooth. Alternatively, put all the ingredients into a food processor or mixer and mix until smooth.

▪

FOLD in the remaining apple, then spoon the cake mixture into the ring mould and level the surface.

▪

MICROWAVE on HIGH for 8–9 minutes or until the cake is well risen, firm to the touch and no longer looks wet around the centre edge. Leave to cool in the dish, then turn out and dredge with the icing sugar.

· CHERRY AND COCONUT CAKE ·

This cake is made by the rubbing-in method, but it is still very quick to prepare. If you find shredded coconut difficult to obtain, add an extra 25 g (1 oz) desiccated coconut instead.

SERVES 8 TO 10

100 g (4 oz) desiccated coconut
25 g (1 oz) shredded coconut
250 g (9 oz) self raising flour
1.25 ml (¼ level tsp) salt
100 g (4 oz) butter or margarine

100 g (4 oz) caster sugar
100 g (4 oz) glacé cherries, finely chopped
2 eggs
300 ml (½ pint) milk

■

GREASE a 1.3 litre (2¼ pint) ring mould and sprinkle with 25 g (1 oz) of the desiccated coconut, spreading any excess evenly in the base of the mould with the shredded coconut.

■

PUT the flour and the salt into a mixing bowl and rub in the butter or margarine until the mixture resembles fine breadcrumbs. Stir in the remaining desiccated coconut, the sugar and cherries.

■

ADD the eggs and milk and beat well, adding more milk if necessary, to make a soft dropping consistency. Spoon the mixture into the prepared dish and smooth the top.

■

COVER and microwave on HIGH for 10–11 minutes until the cake is risen, but still looks slightly moist on the surface.

■

UNCOVER and leave to stand for 10 minutes, then carefully turn out and leave to cool on a wire rack.

· ORANGE YOGURT CAKE ·

Vary this simple cake by using lemon or lime rind and decorate with similar flavoured glacé icing (see page 86).

MAKES 16 SLICES

175 g (6 oz) self raising flour
100 g (4 oz) caster sugar
100 g (4 oz) softened butter or soft tub margarine

finely grated rind of 1 orange
2 eggs
150 ml (¼ pint) natural yogurt

■

GREASE a 1.1 litre (2 pint) ring mould and line the base with a ring of greaseproof paper.

■

PUT all the ingredients into a bowl and beat until smooth. Alternatively, put all the ingredients into a food processor or mixer and mix until smooth.

■

SPOON the mixture into the ring mould and level the surface. Microwave on HIGH for 6–7 minutes or until the cake is well risen, firm to the touch and no longer looks wet around the centre edge. Leave to cool in the dish, then carefully turn out and serve cut into slices.

▪ FRUITED BUTTERSCOTCH RING ▪

Be careful when handling the syrup topping as it gets very hot
– and make sure that you heat it in a heatproof bowl, or it
might melt!

SERVES 10

200 ml (7 fl oz) milk
25 g (1 oz) fresh yeast or 15 ml
    (1 level tbsp) dried yeast and a
    pinch of sugar
400 g (14 oz) strong white flour
5 ml (1 level tsp) salt
40 g (1½ oz) butter or margarine

1 egg, beaten
FOR THE TOPPING
50 g (2 oz) butter or margarine
50 g (2 oz) light soft brown sugar
30 ml (2 tbsp) golden syrup
100 g (4 oz) mixed dried fruit

■

GREASE a 2.3 litre (4 pint) ring mould.

■

PUT the milk in a measuring jug and microwave on HIGH for about 1
minute until the milk is tepid. Add the fresh yeast and stir until it is
dissolved. If using dried yeast and sugar, sprinkle them into the milk and
leave in a warm place for 15 minutes until frothy.

■

SIFT the flour and the salt into a large bowl and microwave on HIGH for
30 seconds to warm the flour. Rub the butter or margarine into the flour.

■

MAKE a well in the centre of the flour and pour in the yeast liquid and the
egg. Mix the ingredients together to form a soft dough.

■

KNEAD the dough on a lightly floured surface for 10 minutes until it
becomes smooth and elastic. Place the dough in a mixing bowl and cover it
with a clean tea-towel. Leave the dough in a warm place for about 1 hour
until it has doubled in size.

■

FOR the topping, put the butter or margarine, sugar and syrup into a
medium ovenproof bowl and microwave on HIGH for 1–2 minutes, stirring
frequently, until melted and boiling. Pour the mixture into the prepared
ring mould and sprinkle half of the dried fruit on top.

■

TURN the risen dough on to a lightly floured surface and knead it again for
about 3 minutes until it becomes smooth. Cut the dough into about twenty-
four small, even pieces and shape them into balls.

■

ARRANGE the balls of dough in the ring mould in loose layers, sprinkling
them with the remaining dried fruit. Cover the dough loosely with a clean
tea-towel and leave it in a warm place until it nearly reaches the top of the
mould.

■

UNCOVER and microwave on HIGH for 5–6 minutes until the ring is well
risen and firm to the touch.

■

LEAVE the Fruited Butterscotch Ring in the mould for 10 minutes before
turning it out to cool on a wire rack.

▪ BATTENBURG CAKE ▪

Impress your family with this cake which is much easier and
quicker to make than it looks. To make a wall of greaseproof
paper, simply take a piece about 7.5 cm (3 inches) wider than
the cake dish and make a 4 cm (1½ inch) pleat in the centre.
Place in the dish. The paper either side of the pleat will stick
to the greased dish and make a lining while the pleat will stand
upright to make a wall.

SERVES 8 TO 10

175 g (6 oz) softened butter or soft tub
  margarine
175 g (6 oz) caster sugar
few drops of vanilla flavouring
3 eggs, beaten
175 g (6 oz) self raising flour

30–60 ml (2–4 tbsp) milk
30 ml (2 level tbsp) cocoa powder
120 ml (8 level tbsp) apricot jam
225 g (8 oz) marzipan
caster sugar, to dredge

▪

GREASE a shallow 18 × 23 cm (7 × 9 inch) dish. Divide the dish in half
lengthways with a wall of greaseproof paper.

▪

PUT the butter or margarine, caster sugar, vanilla flavouring, eggs, flour and
30 ml (2 tbsp) milk into a bowl and beat until smooth. Alternatively, put the
ingredients into a food processor or mixer and mix until smooth.

▪

SPOON half of the mixture into one side of the prepared dish and level the
surface.

▪

ADD the cocoa powder and a little more milk, if necessary, to the remaining
mixture to make a very soft dropping consistency. Spoon this into the other
side of the prepared dish and level the surface. Microwave on HIGH for 5–6
minutes until well risen, but still looks slightly moist on the surface.

▪

LEAVE to stand for 5 minutes, then carefully turn out and leave to cool on a
wire rack.

▪

TRIM the two sponges to an equal size and cut each in half lengthways.

▪

PUT the apricot jam into a small bowl and microwave on HIGH for
1½–2 minutes, stirring frequently, until hot. Spread one side of one piece of
the vanilla sponge with apricot jam and then place one piece of the chocolate
sponge next to it and press the two firmly together.

▪

SPREAD more jam on top of the two halves and place the remaining two
sponges on top, alternating the colours.

▪

ROLL out the marzipan to an oblong long enough to go around the sponge
cakes. Brush the marzipan with apricot jam and place the sponge cakes in
the centre. Bring the marzipan up over the sides to enclose the sponges, then
turn the cake over so the join is underneath.

▪

PRESS the marzipan firmly around the sponges to seal. Trim each end neatly.
Use a small knife to decorate the top of the cake with a criss-cross pattern.
Pinch the top side edges between thumb and forefinger to give a fluted edge.
Dredge lightly with caster sugar and place on a serving dish.

Rum Savarin (page 35), *Cream Slices* (page 54),
Chocolate Roll (page 43)

▪ VICTORIA SANDWICH CAKE ▪

This is the basic cake mixture which has endless variations.
The plain version, as given here, is very pale when cooked,
but if the jam is allowed to ooze out of the sides and the top is
covered with a generous dusting of icing sugar, the cake is
hard to resist.

MAKES 8 TO 10 SLICES

175 g (6 oz) self raising flour
175 g (6 oz) softened butter or soft tub
   margarine
175 g (6 oz) caster sugar

3 eggs
45 ml (3 tbsp) milk
jam, to fill
icing sugar, to dredge

▪

GREASE a deep 20.5 cm (8 inch) round dish and line the base with
greaseproof paper.

▪

PUT the flour, butter or margarine, sugar, eggs and milk into a bowl and beat
until smooth. Alternatively, put all the ingredients into a food processor or
mixer and mix until smooth.

▪

SPOON the mixture into the prepared dish. Cover, stand on a roasting rack
and microwave on HIGH for 6–7 minutes or until risen, slightly shrunk
away from the sides of the dish and a skewer inserted into the centre comes
out clean.

▪

UNCOVER and leave to stand for 5 minutes, then turn out and leave to cool
on a wire rack.

▪

WHEN completely cold, cut in half horizontally, then sandwich together
with jam, and dredge generously with icing sugar.

VARIATIONS

Chocolate Replace 45 ml (3 level tbsp) flour with 45 ml (3 level tbsp) cocoa
powder. Sandwich the cakes with Vanilla or Chocolate butter cream (see
page 87).

Coffee Add 10 ml (2 level tsp) instant coffee granules dissolved in a little
warm water to the creamed butter and sugar mixture with the eggs, or use
10 ml (2 tsp) coffee essence. Sandwich the cakes with Vanilla or Coffee butter
cream (see page 87).

Orange or lemon Add the finely grated rind of an orange or lemon to the
mixture. Sandwich the cakes together with Orange or Lemon butter cream
(see page 87).

*Rich Fruit Cake (page 18), Wholemeal Yogurt Scones (page 74),
Victoria Sandwich Cake (above)*

· RICH FRUIT CAKE ·

This is a very moist cake packed with fruit. It is essential to store it for at least one day before cutting to allow the cake to firm slightly and prevent it from crumbling. Wrapped tightly in greaseproof paper and foil, it will keep for 1–2 weeks.

SERVES 12 TO 16

700 g (1½ lb) mixed dried fruit
50 g (2 oz) glacé cherries, quartered
175 g (6 oz) dark soft brown sugar
5 ml (1 level tsp) ground mixed spice
100 g (4 oz) butter or margarine

300 ml (½ pint) stout
50 g (2 oz) ground almonds
275 g (10 oz) self raising flour
2 eggs
8 walnut halves, to decorate

■

GREASE a deep 20 cm (8 inch) round dish and line the base with greaseproof paper.

■

PUT the fruit, cherries, sugar, spice, butter or margarine and stout into a large bowl and microwave on LOW for 5 minutes.

■

BEAT in the almonds, flour and then the eggs. Beat thoroughly together and pour into the dish. Level the surface and decorate with the walnut halves.

■

STAND on roasting rack and microwave on HIGH for 5 minutes, then on LOW for a further 34–36 minutes or until firm to the touch and a skewer inserted into the centre comes out clean.

■

LEAVE to cool in the dish, then turn out, wrap in greaseproof paper and foil and store for one day before cutting.

· ALMOND AND CHERRY CAKE ·

The ground almonds in this cake make it very rich and moist – and high in calories! If your glacé cherries are covered in a heavy syrup, wash and dry them thoroughly first.

SERVES 10 TO 12

275 g (10 oz) glacé cherries
65 g (2½ oz) self raising flour
225 g (8 oz) softened butter or soft tub margarine
225 g (8 oz) caster sugar

6 eggs, beaten
175 g (6 oz) ground almonds
2.5 ml (½ tsp) almond flavouring
icing sugar, to decorate

■

GREASE a 2.3 litre (4 pint) ring mould.

■

DUST the cherries lightly with 15 g (½ oz) of the flour and arrange them in the bottom of the dish.

■

PUT the butter or margarine and sugar into a large bowl and beat together until they are pale and fluffy. Beat in the eggs, a little at a time, adding a little of the flour if the mixture shows signs of curdling.

■

SIFT in the remaining flour. Add the almonds and almond flavouring and mix the ingredients together well.

■

CAREFULLY spoon the mixture on top of the cherries in the prepared dish and smooth the top.

■

COVER and microwave on HIGH for 13–14 minutes until the cake is risen and a skewer inserted into the centre comes out clean.

■

UNCOVER and leave the cake in the dish until it is cold. Loosen around the sides of the cake with a palette knife and carefully turn it out on to a serving plate. Sift icing sugar over the top.

▪ GINGERBREAD ▪

This dark, rich gingerbread is best eaten after it has matured for 1–2 days, but can be eaten as soon as it is baked if you can't wait!

SERVES 8

100 g (4 oz) butter or margarine
100 g (4 oz) treacle
100 g (4 oz) dark soft brown sugar
150 ml (¼ pint) milk
2 eggs
225 g (8 oz) plain wholemeal flour

5 ml (1 level tsp) ground mixed spice
10 ml (2 level tsp) ground ginger
1.25 ml (¼ level tsp) bicarbonate of soda
30 ml (2 tbsp) stem ginger, finely chopped (optional)

■

GREASE a 1.7 litre (3 pint) loaf dish and line the base with greaseproof paper.

■

PUT the butter or margarine, treacle, sugar and milk in a large bowl and microwave on HIGH for 4 minutes until the butter or margarine is melted. Stir until the sugar is dissolved, then cool slightly.

■

BEAT in the eggs, flour, spices, bicarbonate of soda and chopped ginger, if liked. Pour into the prepared dish, cover and microwave on MEDIUM for 9–11 minutes or until firm and a skewer inserted into the centre comes out clean.

■

UNCOVER and leave to stand until just warm, then turn out on to a wire rack to cool completely. Wrap in foil and store for 1–2 days before eating.

▪ WALNUT AND CHOCOLATE CHIP CAKE ▪

If you cannot find chocolate dots, use the same quantity of
chocolate and cut it into very small pieces.

MAKES 8 TO 10 SLICES

175 g (6 oz) softened butter or soft tub
　margarine
100 g (4 oz) self raising flour
50 g (2 oz) self raising wholemeal
　flour
100 g (4 oz) caster sugar
3 eggs

15 ml (1 tbsp) milk
50 g (2 oz) chocolate dots
50 g (2 oz) walnut halves, chopped
FOR THE FILLING
1 quantity Butter cream (see page 87)
few walnut halves, to decorate

▪

GREASE a deep 20.5 cm (8 inch) round dish and line the base with
greaseproof paper.

▪

PUT the butter or margarine, flours, sugar, eggs and milk into a bowl and
beat until smooth. Alternatively, put all the ingredients into a food
processor or mixer and mix until smooth. Stir in the chocolate dots and
chopped walnuts.

▪

POUR into the prepared dish and level the surface. Stand on a roasting rack,
cover and microwave on HIGH for 6–7 minutes or until risen and a skewer
inserted into the centre comes out clean. Leave to stand for 10 minutes, then
turn out and leave to cool on a wire rack.

▪

WHEN the cake is completely cold, cut in half horizontally and sandwich
together with half of the Butter cream. Spread the remainder on top and
decorate with walnut halves.

▪ CARROT CAKE ▪

This is the ideal cake for cooking in the microwave as the
carrots keep it very moist. Grate the carrots finely or the
texture of the cooked cake will be spoilt by lumps of raw
carrot.

SERVES 6 TO 8

100 g (4 oz) softened butter or soft tub
　margarine
100 g (4 oz) dark soft brown sugar
2 eggs
grated rind and juice of 1 lemon
5 ml (1 level tsp) ground cinnamon
2.5 ml ($\frac{1}{2}$ level tsp) ground nutmeg
2.5 ml ($\frac{1}{2}$ level tsp) ground cloves
15 g ($\frac{1}{2}$ oz) shredded coconut

100 g (4 oz) carrots, peeled and finely
　grated
40 g (1$\frac{1}{2}$ oz) ground almonds
100 g (4 oz) self raising wholemeal
　flour
FOR THE TOPPING
75 g (3 oz) full fat soft cheese
50 g (2 oz) icing sugar
15 ml (1 tbsp) lemon juice
25 g (1 oz) walnuts, chopped

▪

GREASE a 1.6 litre (2$\frac{3}{4}$ pint) ring mould.

▪

Put the butter or margarine and the sugar into a bowl and beat together until pale and fluffy. Add the eggs one at a time, beating well after each addition. Beat in the lemon rind and juice, spices, coconut and carrots. Fold in the ground almonds and the flour.

■

Spoon the mixture into the prepared mould and level the surface. Cover and microwave on HIGH for 10 minutes. When the cake is cooked it will shrink slightly away from the sides of the mould and be firm to the touch.

■

Uncover and leave to stand for 10 minutes, then turn out and leave to cool on a wire rack.

■

When the cake is completely cold, beat together the cheese, icing sugar and lemon juice and spread it evenly over the cake, then sprinkle with the walnuts.

· MARMALADE CAKE ·

A microwave cake dish or ovenproof soufflé dish is ideal for this cake. Be careful when turning it out as it is very fragile; putting it on a tea-towel prevents the wire rack cutting into the crust.

SERVES 8

100 g (4 oz) self raising flour
100 g (4 oz) softened butter or soft tub
  margarine
50 g (2 oz) caster sugar
2 eggs

75 ml (5 level tbsp) chunky orange
  marmalade
FOR THE ORANGE ICING
100 g (4 oz) icing sugar
finely grated rind of 1 orange

■

Grease a deep 20.5 cm (8 inch) round dish and line the base with greaseproof paper.

■

Put the flour, butter or margarine, sugar, eggs and marmalade into a bowl and beat together until smooth and glossy.

■

Spoon the mixture into the dish and level the surface. Stand on a roasting rack, cover and microwave on HIGH for 5–6 minutes until risen and a skewer inserted into the centre comes out clean.

■

Uncover and leave to stand for 5 minutes, then turn out on to a wire rack covered with a clean tea-towel and leave to cool.

■

When the cake is cold make the icing. Sift the icing sugar into a bowl and mix in the orange rind. Gradually add 15 ml (1 tbsp) hot water and beat together. The icing should be thick enough to coat the back of a spoon.

■

Pour the icing over the cake letting it run down the sides. Leave until set.

· LEMON AND HAZELNUT CAKE ·

Hazelnuts add colour and a good nutty texture to this very light, lemony cake. Fill with Continental butter cream if you prefer (see page 88).

SERVES 8

100 g (4 oz) softened butter or soft tub margarine
150 g (5 oz) caster sugar
finely grated rind and juice of 1 lemon
2 eggs, beaten

75 g (3 oz) self raising flour
50 g (2 oz) ground hazelnuts
30 ml (2 tbsp) milk
FOR THE FILLING
300 ml (½ pint) double cream

■

GREASE a deep 20.5 cm (8 inch) round dish and line the base with greaseproof paper.

■

PUT the butter or margarine, 100 g (4 oz) of the sugar, the lemon rind, eggs, flour, half of the hazelnuts and the milk into a bowl and beat together until smooth. Alternatively, put the ingredients into a food processor or mixer and mix until smooth.

■

SPOON the mixture into the prepared dish and smooth the top. Microwave on HIGH for 4–5 minutes or until risen, but still looks slightly moist on the surface.

■

LEAVE to stand for 10 minutes, then turn out on to a wire rack.

■

MIX the lemon juice with the remaining caster sugar. Pour over the top of the cake while still warm and sprinkle with the remaining hazelnuts. Leave to cool completely.

■

WHIP the cream until stiff. Cut the cake in half horizontally, then sandwich together with the cream.

• STICKY TREACLE SPICE CAKE •

This cake really lives up to its name – if you don't like sticky
fingers, eat it with a fork! Make sure you set your cooker to
the correct power level (see page 12) as it is important that the
cake cooks slowly.

MAKES 16 SQUARES

100 g (4 oz) softened butter or soft tub
  margarine
100 g (4 oz) caster sugar
350 g (12 oz) black treacle
1 egg, beaten
275 g (10 oz) plain flour
7.5 ml (1½ level tsp) bicarbonate of
  soda

5 ml (1 level tsp) ground cinnamon
1.25 ml (¼ level tsp) ground ginger
1.25 ml (¼ level tsp) ground cloves
5 ml (1 level tsp) ground mixed spice
2.5 ml (½ level tsp) salt

■

GREASE a 23 cm (9 inch) square dish and line the base with greaseproof
paper

■

PUT the butter or margarine and the sugar into a bowl and beat together
until pale and fluffy, then beat in the treacle. Add the egg, a little at a time,
beating well after each addition.

■

SIFT together the flour, bicarbonate of soda, ground cinnamon, ginger,
cloves, mixed spice and the salt, then beat into the creamed mixture
alternately with 225 ml (8 fl oz) boiling water until the mixture is well
blended.

■

POUR the mixture into the prepared dish. Stand on a roasting rack and
microwave on MEDIUM for 16–18 minutes until slightly shrunk away
from the sides, but still looks slightly moist on the surface. Leave to cool in
the dish. Cut into squares to serve.

• FEATHER ICED COFFEE CAKE •

Feather icing is simple to do, but very effective. The secret of success is to draw the skewer through the piped lines of icing before it has a chance to set.

MAKES 8 TO 10 SLICES

225 g (8 oz) self raising flour
175 g (6 oz) softened butter or soft tub
    margarine
5 ml (1 level tsp) baking powder
175 g (6 oz) light soft brown sugar
3 eggs
30 ml (2 level tbsp) instant coffee
    granules

150 ml (¼ pint) soured cream
FOR THE FILLING
1 quantity coffee flavoured Butter
    cream (see page 87)
FOR THE ICING
175 g (6 oz) icing sugar
5 ml (1 level tsp) instant coffee
    granules

■

GREASE a deep 20.5 cm (8 inch) round dish and line the base with greaseproof paper.

■

PUT the flour, butter or margarine, baking powder, sugar and eggs into a bowl and beat until smooth. Alternatively, put all of the ingredients in a food processor or mixer and mix until smooth.

■

PUT the coffee granules and 30 ml (2 tbsp) water in a small bowl or cup and microwave on HIGH for 30 seconds or until hot. Stir until the coffee has dissolved, leave to cool slightly, then beat into the cake mixture with the soured cream.

■

SPOON the mixture into the prepared dish and level the surface. Stand the dish on a roasting rack, cover and microwave on HIGH for 8–9 minutes or until risen, slightly shrunk away from the sides of the dish but still looks slightly moist on the surface.

■

UNCOVER and leave to stand for 5 minutes, then turn out and leave to cool on a wire rack.

■

WHEN completely cold, cut the cake in half horizontally and sandwich with the Butter cream.

■

TO make the icing, sieve 100 g (4 oz) of the icing sugar into a bowl and gradually beat in 15–30 ml (1–2 tbsp) warm water to make a coating consistency. Sieve the remaining icing sugar into a small bowl with the coffee granules and gradually add 5–10 ml (1–2 tsp) warm water to make a thick piping consistency. Spoon the coffee icing into a greaseproof paper piping bag (see page 86).

■

COAT the top of the cake with the white icing, then quickly snip the end off the piping bag and pipe parallel lines of coloured icing about 1–2 cm (½–¾ inch) apart on top of the white icing.

■

QUICKLY draw the point of a skewer or a sharp knife across the piped lines, first in one direction, then in the other to make a feather pattern. Leave until the icing is set. This cake is best eaten on the day of making.

▪ CARAWAY SEED CAKE ▪

If you have a citrus zester, use it to remove the orange zest –
its much easier and quicker than peeling with a knife.

MAKES 12 SLICES

100 g (4 oz) softened butter or soft tub
   margarine
100 g (4 oz) caster sugar
2.5 ml (½ tsp) vanilla flavouring
2 eggs, beaten

175 g (6 oz) self raising wholemeal
   flour
10 ml (2 level tsp) caraway seeds
1 large orange
FOR THE ICING
1 quantity Glacé icing (see page 86)

■

GREASE a 1.6 litre (2¾ pint) ring mould and line the base with a circle of
greaseproof paper.

■

PUT the butter or margarine and sugar into a bowl and beat together until
pale and fluffy, then beat in the vanilla flavouring. Add the eggs a little at a
time, beating well after each addition.

■

FOLD in the flour and the caraway seeds.

■

REMOVE the zest from the orange, avoiding any pith and cut it into very thin
strips. Set aside. Squeeze the juice of the orange into the cake mixture and
beat thoroughly together.

■

SPOON the cake mixture into the ring mould and level the surface.
Microwave on HIGH for 6–8 minutes or until well risen and firm to the
touch and still looks slightly moist on the surface.

■

LEAVE to stand for 5 minutes, then turn out on to a wire rack covered with a
clean tea-towel and leave to cool.

■

WHEN the cake is cold, transfer to a serving plate. Make the icing and
drizzle over the cake in a thin stream to make a pattern. Sprinkle with the
orange shreds to decorate.

Cakes for Desserts and Special Occasions

These impressive-looking cakes are nevertheless quick and simple to produce, and they provide the perfect finishing touch to a dinner party menu.

· Apple Cakes ·

Don't use a large egg in this recipe or the mixture will rise up over the sides of the dishes during cooking.

Serves 2

1 medium eating apple, peeled and cored
10 ml (2 level tsp) sultanas
2.5 ml ($\frac{1}{2}$ level tsp) ground cinnamon
25 g (1 oz) softened butter or soft tub margarine

25 g (1 oz) caster sugar
25 g (1 oz) self raising wholemeal flour
1 egg, size 6
2.5 ml ($\frac{1}{2}$ level tsp) icing sugar
thick natural yogurt or cream, to serve

Roughly chop the apple and divide between two 150 ml ($\frac{1}{4}$ pint) ramekin dishes. Sprinkle with the sultanas and half of the cinnamon and mix together. Cover and microwave on HIGH for 2 minutes or until the apple is slightly softened.

Meanwhile, put the butter or margarine, sugar, flour and egg into a bowl and beat together until smooth and glossy. Spoon on top of the apples and level the surfaces.

Microwave on HIGH for 2–3 minutes or until slightly shrunk away from the sides of the dishes but still slightly moist on the surface.

Leave to stand for 5 minutes, then turn out on to two serving plates. Mix the remaining cinnamon with the icing sugar and sift over the cakes. Serve immediately with thick natural yogurt or cream.

▪ LEMON GÂTEAU SLICE ▪

The small containers used to cook this cake are available in
disposable microware, sold in packs of six at microware
stockists.

SERVES 2

50 g (2 oz) softened butter or soft tub
  margarine
50 g (2 oz) self raising flour
50 g (2 oz) light soft brown sugar
1 egg, beaten
finely grated rind of ½ lemon

FOR THE FILLING
75 g (3 oz) low fat soft cheese
30 ml (2 tbsp) single cream
15 ml (1 level tbsp) icing sugar
juice of ½ lemon
30 ml (2 tbsp) lemon curd

LINE the bases of two 7.5 × 11 cm (3 × 4½ inch), ovenproof containers with
greaseproof paper.

PUT the butter or margarine, flour, sugar, egg and lemon rind into a bowl
and beat until smooth and glossy.

SPOON into the prepared containers. Cover with absorbent kitchen paper
and microwave on HIGH for 1–2 minutes or until the cakes are risen but
still look slightly moist on the surface. Rearrange the cakes once during
cooking. Leave to stand for 5 minutes, then turn out and leave to cool on a
wire rack.

MEANWHILE, make the filling. Beat the cheese, cream and icing sugar
together with half of the lemon juice. When the cakes are cool, spread one
with 15 ml (1 tbsp) of the lemon curd. Spread half of the cream cheese
mixture on top of the lemon curd, then sandwich the two cakes together.
Swirl the remaining cream cheese mixture on top of the cake.

PUT the remaining lemon curd and the remaining lemon juice in a small
bowl and microwave on HIGH for 10 seconds until just melted but not hot.
Beat together, then drizzle on top of the cake to make a decorative pattern.
Cut the gâteau in half to serve.

· DARK CHOCOLATE CAKE ·

This microwave version of a Continental Sachertorte will not rise much during cooking – it is nevertheless rich, moist and very satisfying.

SERVES 12

100 g (4 oz) plain chocolate, broken into small pieces
100 g (4 oz) softened butter or soft tub margarine
100 g (4 oz) caster sugar
100 g (4 oz) ground almonds
4 eggs, separated

50 g (2 oz) fresh brown breadcrumbs
1 quantity Apricot glaze (see page 89)
FOR THE ICING
200 g (7 oz) plain chocolate, broken into small pieces
200 ml (7 fl oz) double cream

■

GREASE a deep 25.5 cm (10 inch) round dish and line the base with greaseproof paper.

■

PUT the chocolate into a small bowl and microwave on LOW for 4–5 minutes. Stir until melted.

■

CREAM the butter or margarine and sugar together until light and fluffy. Stir in the almonds, egg yolks, breadcrumbs and melted chocolate and beat until well mixed.

■

WHISK the egg whites until stiff, and fold half into the chocolate mixture, then fold in the other half. Pour into the prepared dish and level the surface.

■

MICROWAVE on MEDIUM for 10–11 minutes until shrinking away from the edges and firm in the centre.

■

LEAVE to cool in the dish, then turn out on to a wire rack and brush all over with the apricot glaze.

■

TO make the icing, put the chocolate and the cream into a bowl and microwave on LOW for 6–7 minutes stirring occasionally until the chocolate melts. Do not allow the mixture to boil.

■

MIX well together, then pour the icing all at once on to the top of the cake allowing it to run down the sides. If necessary, use a palette knife to spread the icing over the sides of the cake.

■

LEAVE in a cool place, not the refrigerator, until set. Transfer to a large flat plate to serve.

▪ BLACK FOREST GÂTEAU ▪

Everbody's favourite cake, made here in a third of the time
traditionally required.

SERVES 8 TO 10

two 425 g (15 oz) cans black cherries
45 ml (3 tbsp) kirsch
3 eggs
175 g (6 oz) caster sugar
175 g (6 oz) self raising flour

25 g (1 oz) cocoa powder
5 ml (1 level tsp) baking powder
600 ml (1 pint) double cream
100 g (4 oz) chocolate curls
fresh or canned cherries, to decorate

GREASE a deep 20.5 cm (8 inch) round dish and line the base with
greaseproof paper.

DRAIN the cherries, reserving 45 ml (3 tbsp) juice. Put the cherries with the
juice and the kirsch in a bowl and leave to macerate while making the cake.

PUT the eggs and sugar into a large bowl and whisk until thick enough to
leave a trail on the surface when the whisk is lifted.

SIFT the flour, cocoa powder and baking powder into the mixture and
lightly fold in with a metal spoon. Fold in 75 ml (5 tbsp) hot water. Pour the
mixture into the prepared dish.

STAND on a roasting rack, cover and microwave on HIGH for 5–6 minutes
or until risen and a skewer inserted into the centre comes out clean.

UNCOVER and leave to stand for 5 minutes then turn out and leave to cool
on a wire rack.

CUT the cake horizontally into three. Place a layer on a flat plate and spoon
over 30 ml (2 tbsp) of the cherry juice and kirsch mixture.

WHIP the cream until it holds its shape and spread a little thinly over the
soaked sponge. Top with another layer of sponge and sprinkle with 30 ml
(2 tbsp) of the juice and kirsch mixture. Spread with a layer of cream and
cover with the cherries.

PLACE the remaining layer of sponge on top and sprinkle with the remaining
kirsch and cherry juice.

SPREAD a thin layer of cream around the sides of the cake, reserving a little
to decorate. Press the chocolate curls around the outside of the gâteau.

SPOON the remaining cream into a piping bag fitted with a large star nozzle.
Pipe whirls of cream around the top edge of the gâteau. Decorate with the
fresh or canned cherries.

▪ BANANA AND PASSION FRUIT UPSIDEDOWN CAKE ▪

The mashed banana makes this cake very moist. It is best eaten while still warm.

SERVES 2

25 g (1 oz) softened butter or soft tub margarine
25 g (1 oz) light soft brown sugar
25 g (1 oz) self raising wholemeal flour

1.25 ml (¼ level tsp) ground mixed spice
1 egg, beaten
1 medium ripe banana
15 ml (1 tbsp) clear honey
1 ripe passion fruit

▪

LINE the base of a 7.5 × 11 cm (3 × 4½ inch) ovenproof dish with greaseproof paper.

▪

PUT the butter or margarine, sugar, flour, mixed spice and the egg into a medium bowl and beat together until smooth and glossy.

▪

CUT half of the banana into thin slices and arrange in the base of the prepared dish. Mash the remaining banana and stir into the sponge mixture. Beat together well.

▪

SPOON the mixture on top of the banana slices and cover with absorbent kitchen paper. Microwave on HIGH for 2–2½ minutes or until slightly shrunk away from the sides of the dish but still looks slightly moist on the surface. Leave to stand, covered, for 5 minutes, then turn out on to a serving plate.

▪

PUT the honey into a ramekin dish or cup. Halve the passion fruit and spoon the pulp into the dish with the honey. Microwave on HIGH for 15–30 seconds or until warmed through. Spoon over the cake and serve warm, cut in half.

• COFFEE, RUM AND HAZELNUT GÂTEAU •

Don't worry if this cake rises up very high and then sinks
during cooking – it is quite normal.

SERVES 12

175 g (6 oz) hazelnuts
4 eggs
30 ml (2 tbsp) chicory and coffee
  essence
100 g (4 oz) caster sugar
75 g (3 oz) self raising flour
25 g (1 oz) cornflour

45 ml (3 tbsp) sunflower oil
15–30 ml (1–2 tbsp) dark rum
FOR THE ICING AND DECORATION
double quantity Continental butter
  cream (see page 88)
icing sugar, to dredge

■

GREASE a deep 20.5 cm (8 inch) round dish and line the base with
greaseproof paper.

■

SPREAD the hazelnuts out on a microwave baking tray and microwave on
HIGH for 2 minutes. Turn them on to a clean tea-towel and rub vigorously
to remove the skins. Return them to the baking tray and microwave on
HIGH for 4–5 minutes until lightly browned. Leave to cool, then chop
roughly.

■

MEANWHILE, put the eggs, chicory and coffee essence and sugar into a large
bowl and whisk with an electric whisk until very thick and creamy and the
mixture leaves a trail when the whisk is lifted.

■

SIFT the flours together, then sift into the egg mixture. Fold in lightly using a
metal spoon.

■

GRADUALLY sprinkle on the oil, one tablespoon at a time, and fold in very
lightly using the metal spoon. Pour into the prepared dish.

■

STAND on a roasting rack and microwave on MEDIUM for 7–8 minutes
until well risen, but still slightly moist on the surface. Leave to stand for
10 minutes, then turn out on to a wire rack covered with a clean tea-towel
and leave to cool.

■

WHEN the cake is cool, split in half horizontally and sprinkle with the rum.
Sandwich the cakes together with some of the butter cream and use the rest
to coat the sides and top of the cake.

■

To decorate, press the chopped hazelnuts around the sides of the cake and
on to the top. Dredge the top and sides of the cake with icing sugar.

· LEMON CHEESECAKE ·

This cheesecake can be varied by adding grated orange or lime
rind instead of lemon.

SERVES 6

75 g (3 oz) butter or margarine, cut
    into small pieces
175 g (6 oz) digestive biscuits, finely
    crushed
15 ml (1 level tbsp) gelatine
finely grated rind and juice of 1 lemon
225 g (8 oz) cottage cheese, sieved
150 ml (¼ pint) soured cream

75 g (3 oz) caster sugar
2 eggs, separated
fresh fruit in season such as
    strawberries, sliced; black and
    green grapes, halved and seeded; or
    kiwi fruit, skinned and sliced, to
    decorate

■

PUT the butter or margarine into a bowl and microwave on HIGH for
1–2 minutes until melted. Mix in the biscuit crumbs. Press into the base of a
20.5 cm (8 inch) loose-bottomed or spring-release cake tin. Chill in the
refrigerator for 30 minutes.

■

SPRINKLE the gelatine in 60 ml (4 tbsp) water in a small bowl and microwave
on HIGH for 1 minute, stir until dissolved, then leave to cool slightly.

■

PUT the lemon rind and juice, cottage cheese, soured cream, sugar and the
egg yolks into a bowl and beat together. Stir in the gelatine.

■

WHISK the egg whites until stiff and then fold lightly into the mixture.
Carefully pour into the tin on top of the biscuit base and chill for several
hours, preferably overnight.

■

REMOVE the cheesecake from the tin and place on a flat serving plate.
Decorate with fresh fruit.

· PEACH CHEESECAKE ·

Instead of a crunchy base, this cheesecake has a soft sponge
base which is spooned on top of the cheese mixture before
cooking. To prevent it sinking into the cheese, place
teaspoonfuls of sponge mixture all over the top and then
spread carefully with a knife.

SERVES 12

3 ripe peaches, skinned and stones
    removed
450 g (1 lb) curd cheese
50 g (2 oz) caster sugar
15 ml (1 tbsp) lemon juice
2 eggs
15 ml (1 level tbsp) cornflour
300 ml (½ pint) soured cream

FOR THE BASE
50 g (2 oz) self raising flour
50 g (2 oz) softened butter or soft tub
    margarine
50 g (2 oz) light soft brown sugar
1 egg
15 ml (1 tbsp) milk

■

GREASE a deep 20.5 cm (8 inch) round dish and line the base with
greaseproof paper. Grease the paper.

■

Black Forest Gâteau (page 29), Strawberry Gâteau (page 34),
Coffee, Rum and Hazelnut Gâteau (page 31)

ROUGHLY chop the peaches. Place half in a blender or food processor with the cheese, sugar, lemon juice, eggs, cornflour and half of the cream. Mix until smooth. Stir in the remaining chopped peach, then pour into the prepared dish and level the surface.

∎

PUT the ingredients for the base into a bowl and beat together until smooth. Spoon carefully on top of the peach mixture, then level with a palette knife being careful not to disturb the cheese mixture.

∎

STAND on a roasting rack and microwave on MEDIUM for 20 minutes until a skewer inserted in the centre comes out clean and the sponge mixture on top is risen. (The sponge will look very moist at this stage.)

∎

LEAVE to stand for 15 minutes, then loosen around the sides with a palette knife and carefully turn out on to a flat serving plate so that the sponge base is at the bottom. Peel off the greaseproof paper. (If the cheesecake is still not quite cooked in the centre, return it to the oven, on the serving plate and microwave on MEDIUM for 1–2 minutes until set.)

∎

SPREAD the remaining soured cream on top. Leave until cool, then chill in the refrigerator for 2–3 hours or overnight before serving.

∎ FRESH FRUIT SPONGE FLAN ∎

There's no need to use commercially prepared flan cases when this one can be cooked in only 2 minutes.

SERVES 6

2 eggs
25 g (1 oz) caster sugar
40 g (1½ oz) self raising flour
fresh fruit in season, such as peaches,
    nectarines, grapes, strawberries

½ quantity of Apricot glaze (see
    page 89)
whipped cream, to serve

∎

GREASE a 20.5 cm (8 inch) flan dish and line the centre with a circle of greaseproof paper.

∎

PUT the eggs and sugar into a large bowl and whisk until pale and creamy and thick enough to leave a trail on the surface when the whisk is lifted.

∎

SIFT the flour over the mixture and fold it in very lightly using a large metal spoon. Pour the mixture into the prepared dish.

∎

MICROWAVE on HIGH for 2 minutes until well risen and firm to the touch. Leave to stand for 5 minutes, then turn out on to a wire rack covered with a clean tea-towel and leave to cool.

∎

WHEN cold, transfer the flan case to a serving plate. Arrange the fresh fruit in the flan case and brush with Apricot glaze. Serve as soon as possible, with whipped cream.

Dark Chocolate Cake (page 28), *Microwave Meringues* (page 36), *Lemon Cheesecake* (page 32)

▪ STRAWBERRY GÂTEAU ▪

Ground rice gives this sponge a pleasant crunchy texture.

SERVES 8

FOR THE SHORTBREAD BASE
50 g (2 oz) plain flour
25 g (1 oz) ground rice
50 g (2 oz) butter or margarine
25 g (1 oz) caster sugar
FOR THE SPONGE
175 g (6 oz) self raising flour
5 ml (1 level tsp) baking powder
175 g (6 oz) caster sugar
200 g (7 oz) softened butter or soft tub
  margarine

50 g (2 oz) ground rice
60 ml (4 tbsp) milk
3 eggs
FOR THE DECORATION
45 ml (3 tbsp) strawberry jam
300 ml ($\frac{1}{2}$ pint) double cream
75–100 g (3–4 oz) toasted flaked
  almonds
225 g (8 oz) strawberries

▪

GREASE a 20.5 cm (8 inch) round loose-bottomed dish and a deep 20.5 cm
(8 inch) round dish. Line the base of the deep dish with greaseproof paper.

▪

To make the base, put the flour and ground rice into a bowl and rub in the
butter or margarine until the mixture resembles fine breadcrumbs. Stir in
the sugar and knead together to form a firm dough.

▪

PRESS the mixture into the shallow dish and level the surface with the back
of a teaspoon. Prick all over with a fork, then microwave on HIGH for
2–3 minutes or until the surface of the shortbread just puffs up all over and
begins to look dry. Leave to cool.

▪

PUT all of the sponge ingredients into a bowl and beat until smooth.
Alternatively, put all the ingredients into a food processor or mixer and mix
until smooth.

▪

POUR the mixture into the deep cake dish and level the surface. Stand on a
roasting rack and microwave on HIGH for 6–7 minutes or until risen and a
skewer inserted into the centre comes out clean. Leave to stand for
5 minutes, then turn out on to a wire rack and leave to cool.

▪

WHEN the cake is cool place the shortbread base on a flat serving plate and
spread with the jam. Place the cake on the shortbread. Whip the cream until
stiff and spread a little around the sides of the cake. Coat in the nuts.

▪

SPREAD or pipe the remaining cream on top of the cake and decorate with
the strawberries.

▪ RUM SAVARIN ▪

This classic recipe converts very successfully to microwave
cooking because basting with the rum syrup ensures that the
savarin stays moist. Be very careful when making the sugar
syrup – if the sugar is not completely dissolved before the
mixture boils it will crystallise.

SERVES 10 TO 12

90 ml (6 tbsp) milk
225 g (8 oz) strong white flour
pinch of salt
one sachet easy blend yeast
30 ml (2 level tbsp) caster sugar
100 g (4 oz) softened butter or soft tub
  margarine
4 eggs, beaten
fresh fruit such as apricots, oranges,

peaches, cherries, plums, grapes,
  bananas, apples, pineapple, to fill
150 ml (¼ pint) whipping cream, to
  decorate
FOR THE RUM SYRUP
100 g (4 oz) granulated sugar
100 g (4 oz) light soft brown sugar
60 ml (4 tbsp) dark rum

GREASE a 1.6 litre (2¾ pint) ring mould.

PUT the milk in a jug and microwave on HIGH for 1 minute until just warm.

SIFT the flour and salt into a large bowl and add the yeast, caster sugar,
butter or margarine, eggs and warm milk and beat well for 3–4 minutes.
Alternatively, put all the ingredients into a food processor or mixer and mix
for 2 minutes.

POUR into the prepared ring mould, cover with a clean tea-towel and leave
to rise in a warm place for about 30 minutes until the batter rises three-
quarters of the way up the dish.

UNCOVER and microwave on HIGH for 6 minutes until well risen and firm
to the touch. Leave to stand for 5 minutes, then turn out into a shallow
serving dish.

PUT the sugars for the syrup into a large bowl and add 450 ml (¾ pint) water.
Microwave on HIGH for 2 minutes, stirring occasionally until the sugar has
dissolved. Microwave on HIGH until boiling, then for at least 10 minutes or
until the syrup becomes fairly thick.

STIR in the rum and pour over the savarin. Leave to cool completely,
occasionally basting the savarin with any excess syrup. To serve, fill the
centre with fresh fruit and decorate with whipped cream.

▪ MICROWAVE MERINGUES ▪

This mixture puffs up and makes delicate meringues which
can be sandwiched together with cream or Continental butter
cream (see page 88). It makes rather a lot – if you prefer, some
of the mixture may be tightly wrapped and stored in the
refrigerator for about 2 weeks.

MAKES 32

1 egg white
about 275–300 g (10–11 oz) icing
  sugar
FLAVOURINGS *(optional)*
15 ml (1 level tbsp) cocoa powder
or 5 ml (1 level tsp) instant coffee

granules dissolved in 2.5 ml ($\frac{1}{2}$ tsp)
  boiling water
or a few drops almond essence
FOR THE FILLING
fresh fruit
whipped cream

▪

PUT the egg white into a small bowl and whisk lightly with a fork. Gradually
sift in the icing sugar and the cocoa, if using, and mix to give a very firm, non
sticky but pliable dough, similar to a fondant mixture.

▪

IF using other flavourings, stir in and add a little more icing sugar if
necessary to retain a firm paste.

▪

DIVIDE the mixture into 32, then roll into balls. Place a sheet of greaseproof
paper in the base of the cooker or on the turntable and arrange a quarter of
the balls of paste in a circle on the paper, spacing them well apart.

▪

MICROWAVE on HIGH for 1$\frac{1}{2}$ minutes until the paste has puffed up and
formed meringue-like balls.

▪

CAREFULLY lift the cooked meringues off the paper and transfer to a wire
rack to cool. Repeat three more times with the remaining fondant to make
32 meringues.

▪

JUST before serving sandwich the meringues together with fresh fruit and
cream.

Chocolate Cakes

Chocolate cakes are an all-time favourite, especially with children. Whether you're making a plain chocolate sponge or a rich chocolate mousse cake, they are perfectly suited to microwave baking.

▪ Boston Brownies ▪

These are another American favourite. Watch carefully during cooking to make sure they do not overcook – they should be very moist.

Makes 12 Squares

100 g (4 oz) plain chocolate, broken
  into small pieces
100 g (4 oz) butter or margarine, cut
  into pieces
100 g (4 oz) dark soft brown sugar

100 g (4 oz) self raising flour
10 ml (2 level tsp) cocoa powder
2 eggs
2.5 ml (½ tsp) vanilla flavouring
100 g (4 oz) walnuts, roughly chopped

■

Grease a shallow 18 × 23 cm (7 × 9 inch) dish.

■

Put the chocolate and butter or margarine into a large heatproof bowl. Microwave on LOW for 4–5 minutes. Stir until the chocolate and the butter have melted.

■

Stir in the sugar, flour and cocoa. Add the eggs and vanilla flavouring and beat well to make a smooth batter. Stir in the walnuts.

■

Pour the mixture into the dish, stand on a roasting rack and microwave on HIGH for 4–5 minutes until well risen, firm to the touch, but still slightly moist on the surface.

■

Leave to cool in the dish, then cut into squares before serving.

▪ CHOCOLATE FUDGE CAKE ▪

*Don't worry if the icing is very thin when you remove it from
the microwave – keep beating and as it cools it will thicken.*

SERVES 16

30 ml (2 level tbsp) cocoa powder
75 ml (5 tbsp) milk
150 g (5 oz) softened butter or soft tub
  margarine
150 g (5 oz) light soft brown sugar
2 eggs
150 g (5 oz) self raising flour
5 ml (1 level tsp) baking powder

FOR THE FUDGE TOPPING
100 g (4 oz) light soft brown sugar
100 g (4 oz) plain chocolate, broken
  into small pieces
50 g (2 oz) butter or margarine, cut
  into pieces
45 ml (3 tbsp) double cream

▪

GREASE a 23 cm (9 inch) square dish and line base with greaseproof paper.

▪

PUT the cocoa and the milk into a medium bowl and microwave on HIGH
for 1 minute or until hot. Beat thoroughly to dissolve the cocoa.

▪

ADD the butter or margarine, sugar, eggs, flour and baking powder and beat
thoroughly until smooth and well mixed.

▪

POUR into the prepared dish, stand on a roasting rack and microwave on
MEDIUM for 8–9 minutes until risen and firm to the touch, but still looks
slightly moist on the surface. Leave to cool in the dish.

▪

WHEN the cake is cold, turn out on to a serving plate. To make the fudge
topping, put all the ingredients into a large bowl and microwave on HIGH
for 2 minutes until the butter has melted and the sugar dissolved, stirring
occasionally.

▪

BEAT thoroughly together for 2–3 minutes until the mixture starts to
thicken. Spread evenly on top of the sponge and mark into swirls with a
knife. Leave until set, then cut into squares.

▪ CHOCOLATE LOAF CAKE ▪

*The easiest way to measure golden syrup is to weigh the tin
without the lid, then spoon the syrup directly into a large
mixing bowl until the scales read 100 g (4 oz) lighter.*

SERVES 10

100 g (4 oz) golden syrup
100 g (4 oz) dark soft brown sugar
100 g (4 oz) butter or margarine
175 g (6 oz) self raising flour
50 g (2 oz) cocoa powder
1 egg, beaten

150 ml ($\frac{1}{4}$ pint) milk
100 g (4 oz) plain chocolate, broken
  into small pieces
chocolate caraque, to decorate (see
  page 90)

▪

GREASE a 1.7 litre (3 pint) loaf dish and line the base with greaseproof paper.

▪

PUT the syrup, brown sugar and butter or margarine into a large bowl and
microwave on HIGH for 2 minutes or until the butter has melted and the
sugar dissolved, stirring occasionally.

ADD the flour, cocoa, egg and milk and beat together until smooth and glossy.

SPOON the mixture into the prepared dish and level the surface. Stand on a roasting rack and microwave on HIGH for 5 minutes until risen, but still slightly moist on the surface.

LEAVE to stand for 5 minutes, then turn out and cool on a wire rack.

WHEN the cake is cold, put the chocolate into a small bowl and microwave on LOW for about 4 minutes until melted, stirring occasionally.

SPREAD the melted chocolate over the top of the cake, allowing it to trickle over the edges, decorate with chocolate caraque, then leave to set.

▪ CHOCOLATE MOUSSE CAKE ▪

This cake is really a mousse with a cake base. It is very rich and is the ideal choice when entertaining.

SERVES 8

175 g (6 oz) plain chocolate, broken
  into small pieces
30 ml (2 tbsp) orange-flavoured
  liqueur
25 g (1 oz) butter or margarine
2 eggs
50 g (2 oz) caster sugar
25 g (1 oz) self raising flour

FOR THE MOUSSE TOPPING
225 g (8 oz) plain chocolate, broken
  into small pieces
30 ml (2 tbsp) orange-flavoured
  liqueur
2 eggs
julienne strips of orange rind and
  chocolate curls, to decorate

GREASE a 20 cm (8 inch) round loose-bottomed cake dish.

PUT the chocolate, liqueur and butter for the cake into a bowl. Microwave on LOW for 4–5 minutes until soft. Stir until the chocolate has melted.

USING an electric whisk, whisk the eggs and sugar together until very thick and creamy and the mixture leaves a trail when the whisk is lifted. Carefully fold in the flour, then fold in the melted chocolate mixture.

POUR the mixture into the prepared dish, stand on a roasting rack and microwave on MEDIUM for 8–9 minutes until risen, but still looks slightly moist on the surface. Leave to cool in the dish.

WHEN the cake is cool, make the mouse topping. Put the chocolate into a medium bowl and microwave on LOW for 5–6 minutes until soft. Stir until the chocolate has melted. Stir in the liqueur.

SEPARATE the eggs and beat the egg yolks into the chocolate mixture. Whisk the egg whites until stiff, then carefully fold in.

POUR the mousse over the sponge base and level the surface. Refrigerate overnight.

THE next day, remove the cake carefully from the dish and put on to a serving plate. Arrange strips of orange rind and the chocolate curls around the edge of the cake to decorate.

· CHOCOLATE SANDWICH CAKE ·

Wholemeal flour gives this cake a nutty texture, but if you
prefer, use self raising white flour.

SERVES 8

175 g (6 oz) softened butter or soft tub
   margarine
175 g (6 oz) dark soft brown sugar
3 eggs, beaten
175 g (6 oz) self raising wholemeal
   flour
25 g (1 oz) cocoa powder
about 60 ml (4 tbsp) milk

FOR THE FILLING
175 g (6 oz) icing sugar
75 g (3 oz) softened butter or soft tub
   margarine
40 g (1½ oz) plain chocolate, broken
   into small pieces
15 ml (1 tbsp) milk
chocolate circles, to decorate (see
   page 90)

■

GREASE a deep 20.5 cm (8 inch) round dish and line the base with
greaseproof paper.

■

PUT all the ingredients for the cake, except the milk, into a large bowl and
beat until smooth. Alternatively put all the ingredients into a food
processor or mixer and mix until smooth. Stir in enough milk to give a very
soft dropping consistency.

■

SPOON the mixture into the prepared dish and level the surface. Stand on a
roasting rack, cover and microwave on HIGH for 8–9 minutes until risen
and a skewer inserted into the centre comes out clean. Uncover and leave
the cake to stand in the dish for 5 minutes, then turn out and leave to cool
on a wire rack.

■

To make the filling, gradually sift and beat the sugar into the butter or
margarine.

■

PUT the chocolate into a small bowl and microwave on LOW for
2–2½ minutes until melted. Stir into the butter mixture with the milk and
beat until smooth.

■

CUT the cake in half horizontally and sandwich together with half of the
icing. Swirl the rest of the icing on top of the cake with a palette knife.
Decorate with chocolate circles.

• Chocolate Coffee Refrigerator Slice •

Melting chocolate is easy and convenient in the microwave. Always choose plain chocolate for cooking as milk chocolate contains condensed or powdered milk that separates on heating. Chocolate-flavour cake coverings melt easily but the flavour is not as good.

SERVES 8

30 ml (2 tbsp) instant coffee granules
45 ml (3 tbsp) brandy
100 g (4 oz) plain chocolate, broken into small pieces
50 g (2 oz) icing sugar
100 g (4 oz) softened butter or margarine

2 egg yolks
50 g (2 oz) chopped almonds, toasted
300 ml ($\frac{1}{2}$ pint) whipping cream
about 30 sponge fingers
coffee beans, to decorate

■

GREASE a 1.7 litre (3 pint) loaf dish and line the base with greaseproof paper. Grease the paper.

■

PUT the coffee granules and 200 ml (7 fl oz) water into a small bowl and microwave on HIGH for 2 minutes or until hot. Stir until the coffee is dissolved. Stir in the brandy. Set aside to cool.

■

PUT the chocolate in a medium bowl with 15 ml (1 tbsp) water and microwave on LOW for 2–3 minutes until soft. Stir until the chocolate has melted, then sift in the icing sugar and beat thoroughly together. Add the butter or margarine and the egg yolks, beating well. Stir in the nuts.

■

LIGHTLY whip the cream and stir half of it into the chocolate mixture. Refrigerate the remaining cream.

■

LINE the bottom of the prepared loaf dish with sponge fingers, cutting to fit if necessary. Spoon over one third of the coffee and brandy mixture.

■

CONTINUE layering the chocolate mixture and sponge fingers into the dish, soaking each layer with coffee and ending with soaked sponge fingers. Weight down lightly and refrigerate for 3–4 hours until set.

■

TURN out on to a serving plate, remove the paper and decorate with the reserved whipped cream and the coffee beans.

· MARBLED CHOCOLATE RING CAKE ·

Don't worry if this cake rises up and touches the cover during cooking – it won't spoil the finished appearance of this delicious cake.

SERVES 8

50 g (2 oz) plain chocolate, broken
 into pieces
10 ml (2 level tsp) cocoa powder
100 g (4 oz) butter or margarine
100 g (4 oz) caster sugar
2 eggs
60 ml (4 tbsp) milk
175 g (6 oz) plain flour

5 ml (1 level tsp) baking powder
25 g (1 oz) ground almonds
FOR THE ICING
250 g (9 oz) plain chocolate, broken
 into small pieces
100 g (4 oz) butter or margarine, cut
 into small pieces

■

GREASE a 1.6 litre (2¾ pint) ring mould and line the base with a ring of greaseproof paper. Put the chocolate, the cocoa and 30 ml (2 tbsp) water into a medium bowl and microwave on LOW for 2–3 minutes. Stir until the chocolate has melted.

■

PUT the butter or margarine and the sugar into a bowl and beat together until pale and fluffy. Beat in the eggs one at a time and stir in the milk.

■

FOLD the flour and baking powder into the creamed mixture with the ground almonds. Spoon half of the mixture into the chocolate mixture and mix thoroughly.

■

SPOON alternate tablespoonfuls of the plain and chocolate mixtures into the dish.

■

DRAW a knife through the cake mixture in a spiral to make a marbled effect and level the surface.

■

COVER and microwave on HIGH for 5–6 minutes until well risen and firm to the touch. Leave to stand for 10 minutes, then turn out and leave to cool on a wire rack.

■

To make the icing, put 150 g (5 oz) of the chocolate into a small bowl with 30 ml (2 tbsp) water and the butter or margarine. Microwave on LOW for 2–3 minutes. Stir until the chocolate and butter have melted, then pour over the cake. Using a palette knife, spread the icing to completely coat the top and sides. Leave until set.

■

PUT the remaining chocolate into a small bowl and microwave on LOW for 4–5 minutes. Stir until melted. Spoon immediately into a greaseproof paper piping bag (see page 86), snip off the tip and drizzle chocolate over the cake, to decorate.

▪ CHOCOLATE ROLL ▪

This is the microwave equivalent of a Swiss roll. Make sure
that you have the paper ready to turn the cake on to and that
you roll it up quickly or it will crack.

SERVES 8

2 eggs, beaten
25 g (1 oz) dark soft brown sugar
50 g (2 oz) self raising flour
30 ml (2 level tbsp) cocoa powder

15 ml (1 tbsp) milk
175 g (6 oz) strawberries, hulled
300 ml (½ pint) double cream

■

LINE the base of a shallow 23 cm (9 inch) square dish with greaseproof
paper.

■

PUT the eggs and sugar into a medium bowl and whisk until pale and creamy
and thick enough to leave a trail on the surface when the whisk is lifted.

■

SIFT in the flour and cocoa powder, then fold in using a large metal spoon.
Fold in the milk.

■

POUR the cake mixture into the prepared dish and level the surface. Stand
on a roasting rack, cover loosely with absorbent kitchen paper and
microwave on HIGH for 2½–3 minutes until slightly shrunk away from the
sides of the dish, but still looks slightly moist on the surface. Leave to stand
for 5 minutes.

■

MEANWHILE, place a sheet of greaseproof paper on a flat surface. Turn the
cake out on to the greaseproof paper and roll up with the paper inside.
Leave to cool on a wire rack.

■

SLICE the strawberries and set aside a few slices for decoration. Whip the
cream until just stiff, fold the strawberries into half of the cream and spoon
the remaining cream into a piping bag fitted with a large star nozzle. Unroll
the cake and spread with the strawberry and cream filling. Re-roll and place,
seam side down, on a serving plate.

■

To decorate, pipe rosettes of cream the length of the roll and arrange the
reserved strawberry slices on top. Serve cut into slices.

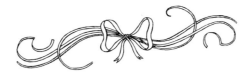

· CHOCOLATE ALMOND CAKE ·

The almond flavour is very subtle, but the ground almonds
add texture and help keep this cake moist.

SERVES 8

100 g (4 oz) softened butter or soft tub
　margarine
100 g (4 oz) caster sugar
2 eggs
45 ml (3 tbsp) clear honey
150 ml (¼ pint) soured cream
100 g (4 oz) self raising flour
40 g (1½ oz) cocoa powder
50 g (2 oz) ground almonds

FOR THE ICING
75 g (3 oz) plain chocolate, broken
　into small pieces
15 ml (1 tbsp) brandy
25 g (1 oz) softened butter or soft tub
　margarine
45 ml (3 tbsp) single cream
50 g (2 oz) flaked almonds, toasted

■

GREASE a deep 20.5 cm (8 inch) round dish and line the base with
greaseproof paper.

■

PUT the butter or margarine and sugar in a bowl and beat together until pale
and fluffy. Gradually beat in the eggs, honey and soured cream. Fold in the
flour, cocoa and ground almonds.

■

SPOON the cake mixture into the prepared dish. Stand on a roasting rack
and microwave on HIGH for 10 minutes until risen, but still looks slightly
moist on the surface. Leave to stand for 5 minutes, then turn out and leave
to cool on a wire rack.

■

TO make the icing, put the chocolate, brandy, butter or margarine and
cream in a small bowl and microwave on LOW for 3 minutes until melted,
stirring once.

■

POUR the icing over the cold cake, allowing it to run down the sides.
Sprinkle with the almonds. Leave until set before serving.

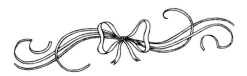

▪ CHOCOLATE CUP CAKES ▪

If you do not have a muffin tray, use suitable china cups to
support the cakes during cooking and arrange them in a circle.

MAKES 18

100 g (4 oz) softened butter or soft tub
  margarine
100 g (4 oz) caster sugar
2 eggs
75 g (3 oz) self raising flour
25 g (1 oz) cocoa powder

30 ml (2 tbsp) milk
FOR THE ICING
100 g (4 oz) plain chocolate, broken
  into small pieces
25 g (1 oz) butter or margarine

■

PUT the butter or margarine, sugar, eggs, flour, cocoa and milk into a bowl
and beat until smooth. Alternatively, put all of the ingredients into a food
processor or mixer and mix until smooth.

■

PUT six double layers of paper cases into a microwave muffin tray. Fill the
cases one-third full with the cake mixture.

■

MICROWAVE on HIGH for 1 minute until the cakes are risen, but still look
slightly moist on the surface. Remove from the muffin tray and leave to cool
on a wire rack. Repeat twice with the remaining mixture to make eighteen
cakes.

■

WHEN the cakes are cool, make the icing. Put the chocolate into a bowl.
Microwave on LOW for 3–4 minutes until melted. Add in the butter or
margarine and stir until melted. Quickly spoon the icing on top of the cakes
to completely cover the surface. Leave until set.

▪ CHOCOLATE CRACKLES ▪

These teatime favourites are easy enough for children to make
themselves, and are especially quick and clean to prepare
when using the microwave.

MAKES 12

225 g (8 oz) plain chocolate, broken
  into small pieces
15 ml (1 tbsp) golden syrup

50 g (2 oz) butter or margarine
50 g (2 oz) cornflakes or rice breakfast
  cereal

■

PUT the chocolate, golden syrup and butter or margarine into a medium
heatproof bowl. Microwave on LOW for 6–7 minutes or until the
chocolate is melted.

■

MIX together, then fold in the cornflakes or rice cereal. When well mixed,
spoon into twelve paper cases or a shallow 20.5 cm (8 inch) round dish and
leave to set. Store in the refrigerator.

· DEVIL'S FOOD CAKE ·

Devil's food cake is the classic dark, rich American cake
covered in white peaked icing. Use the icing immediately after
making as it sets quite quickly.

MAKES 10 TO 12 SLICES

*75 g (3 oz) plain chocolate, broken
into small pieces
10 ml (2 level tsp) instant coffee
granules
15 ml (1 level tbsp) cocoa powder
175 g (6 oz) softened butter or soft tub
margarine
100 g (4 oz) dark soft brown sugar*

*50 g (2 oz) caster sugar
3 eggs
225 g (8 oz) self raising flour
5 ml (1 level tsp) baking powder
150 ml (¼ pint) soured cream*
FOR THE ICING
*double quantity Seven-minute frosting
(see page 88)*

■

GREASE a deep 20.5 cm (8 inch) round dish and line the base with
greaseproof paper.

■

PUT the chocolate, coffee granules and cocoa powder into a bowl with 30 ml
(2 tbsp) water and microwave on HIGH for 1–2 minutes until hot. Stir until
the coffee and cocoa have dissolved. Cool slightly.

■

MEANWHILE, put the remaining ingredients into a bowl and beat until
smooth. Alternatively, put all of the ingredients into a food processor or
mixer and mix until smooth.

■

GRADUALLY beat in the chocolate mixture, then beat thoroughly together.
Pour the mixture into the prepared dish. Cover, stand on a roasting rack
and microwave on HIGH for 8–9 minutes or until risen, slightly shrunk
away from the sides of the dish and a skewer inserted into the centre comes
out clean.

■

UNCOVER and leave to stand for 5 minutes, then turn out and leave to cool
on a wire rack.

■

WHEN the cake is cool, make the Seven-minute frosting. Cut the cake
horizontally into three. Place one layer on a flat plate and spread with a little
of the frosting.

■

PLACE another layer of sponge on top and spread with more of the frosting.
Repeat with the remaining sponge, then quickly cover the cake completely
with the remaining frosting. Using a palette knife, swirl the icing and pull it
up into peaks all over the cake. Leave until set.

▪ RICH CHOCOLATE AND COCONUT SQUARES ▪

Cook the base mixture for these cakes until it just looks dry
and feels firm to the touch.

MAKES 16

25 g (1 oz) caster sugar
25 g (1 oz) cocoa powder
100 g (4 oz) plain flour
50 g (2 oz) softened butter or soft tub
  margarine
1 egg

FOR THE FILLING
300 ml (½ pint) evaporated milk
25 g (1 oz) cocoa powder
50 g (2 oz) porridge oats
50 g (2 oz) desiccated coconut
FOR THE ICING
100 g (4 oz) icing sugar
10 ml (2 level tsp) cocoa powder

■

GREASE a shallow 23 cm (9 inch) square dish.

■

PUT the sugar, cocoa, flour, butter or margarine, egg and 30 ml (2 tbsp)
water into a bowl. Beat thoroughly together to make a stiff paste. Spread in
the base of the dish and level the surface. Microwave on HIGH for
3–4 minutes or until the surface of the mixture looks dry.

■

PUT the ingredients for the filling in a bowl and microwave on HIGH for
4–5 minutes until very thick, stirring occasionally. Spread evenly over the
base and leave to cool.

■

To make the icing, sift the icing sugar into a bowl. Blend the cocoa with
about 15 ml (1 tbsp) hot water, then beat into the icing sugar, adding a little
extra hot water if necessary to make a coating consistency. Spread over
filling. Leave until set, then cut into sixteen squares.

▪ CHOCOLATE BISCUIT CAKE ▪

This is very easy to make and the fruit and nuts can be varied
according to what you have in your cupboard.

MAKES 10 WEDGES

100 g (4 oz) plain chocolate, broken
  into small pieces
15 ml (1 level tbsp) golden syrup
100 g (4 oz) butter or margarine, cut
  into small pieces
30 ml (2 tbsp) double cream

100 g (4 oz) digestive biscuits, roughly
  broken
25 g (1 oz) sultanas
25 g (1 oz) glacé cherries, chopped
50 g (2 oz) walnuts, roughly chopped

■

GREASE an 18 cm (7 inch) flan ring.

■

PUT the chocolate into a large ovenproof bowl with the syrup and the butter
or margarine. Microwave on LOW for 4–5 minutes or until the chocolate
has melted, stirring frequently. Add the remaining ingredients and mix
thoroughly.

■

TURN the mixture into the prepared flan ring and level the top. Mark lightly
into ten wedges, then chill in the refrigerator for 1–2 hours until set.

47

Small Cakes and Pastries

The perfect solution for an impromptu tea, when friends have dropped in unexpectedly, or as a treat to fill the corners of school lunch boxes.

• Butterfly Cakes •

If you do not have a muffin tray, use suitable china cups, arranged in a circle, to support the paper cases.

Makes 18

100 g (4 oz) softened butter or soft tub
    margarine
100 g (4 oz) caster sugar
2 eggs

100 g (4 oz) self raising flour
30 ml (2 tbsp) milk
1 quantity Butter cream (see page 87)
icing sugar, to decorate

■

Put the butter or margarine, sugar, eggs and flour into a large bowl and beat until smooth. Alternatively put the ingredients into a food processor or mixer and mix until smooth. Add the milk to make a soft dropping consistency.

■

Arrange six double layers of paper cases in a microwave muffin tray. Fill the paper cases half-full and microwave on HIGH for 1 minute until risen, but still slightly moist on the surface. Transfer to a wire rack to cool. Repeat twice with the remaining mixture to make eighteen cakes.

■

When the cakes are cold, cut a slice off the top of each one and pipe or fork a generous amount of Butter cream over the surface.

■

Cut each top in half, then replace at an angle in the filling to resemble butterflies' wings. Dust with sifted icing sugar.

· ENGLISH MADELEINES ·

Cook the Madeleines in paper drinking cups – plastic cups
would melt during cooking.

MAKES 8

*100 g (4 oz) softened butter or soft tub
  margarine*
100 g (4 oz) caster sugar
2 eggs
100 g (4 oz) self raising flour

75 ml (5 level tbsp) red jam
40 g (1½ oz) desiccated coconut
*4 glacé cherries, halved, and angelica
  pieces, to decorate*

■

LINE the bases of eight paper drinking cups with rounds of greaseproof
paper.

■

PUT the butter or margarine, sugar, eggs and flour into a bowl and beat until
smooth. Alternatively, put the ingredients into a food processor or mixer
and mix until smooth.

■

DIVIDE the mixture evenly between the prepared cups. Place the cups on
two flat heatproof plates, four on each plate.

■

MICROWAVE on HIGH, one plate at a time, for 1½–2 minutes until risen,
but still slightly moist on the surface. Leave to stand for 1–2 minutes, then
turn out and leave to cool on a wire rack.

■

WHEN the cakes are cold, trim the bases, if necessary, so that they stand
firmly and are about the same height.

■

PUT the jam into a small heatproof bowl and microwave on HIGH for
1–2 minutes until melted. Stir well.

■

SPREAD the coconut out on a large plate. Spear a cake on a skewer or a fork,
brush with the jam and then roll in the coconut until evenly coated. Repeat
with the remaining cakes.

■

TOP each Madeleine with half a glacé cherry and small pieces of angelica.
These are best eaten on the day of making.

• QUEEN CAKES •

If you want to add some colour to these pale cakes, ice them
with Glacé icing (see page 86) and decorate appropriately.

MAKES 18

100 g (4 oz) softened butter or soft tub
   margarine
100 g (4 oz) caster sugar
2 eggs

100 g (4 oz) self raising flour
50 g (2 oz) sultanas
30 ml (2 tbsp) milk

∎

PUT the butter or margarine, sugar, eggs and flour into a large bowl and beat
until smooth. Alternatively, put the ingredients into a food processor or
mixer and mix until smooth. Mix in the sultanas and add the milk to make a
soft dropping consistency.

ARRANGE six double layers of paper cases in a microwave muffin tray. Fill
the prepared paper cases half-full and microwave on HIGH for 1 minute
until risen, but still slightly moist on the surface. Transfer to a wire rack to
cool. Repeat twice with the remaining mixture.

VARIATIONS
Replace the sultanas with one of the following:
50 g (2 oz) chopped dates; 50 g (2 oz) chopped glacé cherries; 50 g (2 oz)
chocolate chips; 50 g (2 oz) chopped crystallised ginger.

• GINGER BUNS •

Ground ginger and light soft brown sugar give these cakes a
pleasant golden colour.

MAKES 18

100 g (4 oz) self raising flour
50 g (2 oz) softened butter or soft tub
   margarine
50 g (2 oz) light soft brown sugar
30 ml (2 tbsp) golden syrup
5 ml (1 level tsp) ground ginger
1 egg

30 ml (2 tbsp) milk
25 g (1 oz) stem ginger, drained and
   finely chopped
FOR THE ICING
100 g (4 oz) icing sugar
stem ginger, thinly sliced

∎

PUT the flour, butter or margarine, sugar, syrup, ginger, egg, and milk into a
bowl and beat until smooth. Alternatively, put all the ingredients into a
food processor or mixer and mix until smooth.

∎

STIR in the chopped stem ginger and mix well together.

∎

ARRANGE six double layers of paper cases in a microwave muffin tray. Put a
heaped teaspoon of the cake mixture into each.

∎

MICROWAVE on HIGH for 1½ minutes or until risen, but still slightly moist
on the surface. Transfer to a wire rack and leave to cool. Repeat twice with
the remaining mixture to make eighteen buns.

∎

WHEN all the buns are cold, make the icing. Sift the icing sugar into a small bowl, then stir in 15–30 ml (1–2 tbsp) hot water and beat thoroughly together to make a coating consistency.

■

SPOON the icing on to the cakes and decorate each with a small piece of stem ginger. Leave until set.

▪ BANANA AND COCONUT BUNS ▪

Shredded coconut looks and tastes better than desiccated coconut in these buns, but if shredded is unavailable desiccated coconut can be used.

MAKES 12

1 ripe banana
50 g (2 oz) caster sugar
50 g (2 oz) self raising flour
50 g (2 oz) softened butter or soft tub
  margarine

1 egg
5 ml (1 tsp) lemon juice
FOR THE TOPPING
100 g (4 oz) icing sugar
50 g (2 oz) shredded coconut

■

PUT the banana, sugar, flour, butter or margarine, egg and lemon juice into a bowl and beat until smooth. Alternatively, put all the ingredients into a food processor or mixer and mix until smooth.

■

ARRANGE six double layers of paper cases in a microwave muffin tray. Divide half the mixture between the paper cases and microwave on HIGH for 2 minutes or until risen, but still slightly moist on the surface. Transfer to a wire rack and leave to cool. Repeat with the remaining mixture to make twelve buns.

■

WHEN all the buns are cold, make the icing. Sift the icing sugar into a small bowl, then stir in 15–30 ml (1–2 tbsp) hot water and beat thoroughly together to make a coating consistency.

■

SPOON the icing on to the cakes and sprinkle generously with the coconut. Leave until set.

• APRICOT AND HONEY SQUARES •

Watch this mixture carefully during cooking – if it overcooks it will be very dry.

MAKES 16

100 g (4 oz) butter or margarine
100 g (4 oz) thick honey
finely grated rind and juice of 1
    orange
75 g (3 oz) no-soak dried apricots,
    finely chopped

175 g (6 oz) self raising flour
2 eggs
FOR THE TOPPING
30 ml (2 tbsp) clear honey
25 g (1 oz) toasted flaked almonds

■

GREASE a shallow 23 cm (9 inch) square dish.

■

PUT the butter or margarine, honey, orange rind and juice and the apricots in a medium bowl. Microwave on HIGH for 2–3 minutes until the butter or margarine has melted.

■

STIR in the remaining ingredients and beat until well mixed. Pour into the dish. Microwave on HIGH for 5–6 minutes until risen but still slightly moist on the surface.

■

COOL slightly, then brush with the clear honey and sprinkle with the almonds. Leave until completely cold, then cut into sixteen squares before serving.

• PEANUT SQUARES •

These rich sponge squares are a firm favourite with children.

MAKES 12

100 g (4 oz) golden syrup
100 g (4 oz) butter or margarine, cut
    into small pieces
225g (8 oz) unsalted peanuts,
    chopped
2 eggs

175 g (6 oz) self raising flour
FOR THE TOPPING
30 ml (2 tbsp) golden syrup
60 ml (4 level tbsp) crunchy peanut
    butter
15 ml (1 tbsp) lemon juice

■

GREASE a shallow 18 × 23 cm (7 × 9 inch) dish.

■

PUT the golden syrup and the butter or margarine into a medium bowl and microwave on HIGH for 2 minutes or until melted.

■

ADD the remaining ingredients, then beat thoroughly together. Spread evenly in the dish.

■

MICROWAVE on HIGH for 5 minutes or until risen and firm to the touch. Put all of the topping ingredients into a small heatproof bowl and microwave on HIGH for 1–2 minutes until the peanut butter is slightly melted. Beat thoroughly together, then pour over the cake.

■

LEAVE until set then cut into twelve squares before serving.

· ALMOND SLICES ·

It is possible to brown almonds in the microwave because
they have a high fat content. The toasted almonds add both
colour and flavour to these delicious slices.

MAKES 16 SLICES

40 g (1½ oz) flaked almonds
FOR THE PASTRY
175 g (6 oz) plain flour
pinch of salt
75 g (3 oz) butter or margarine
FOR THE FILLING
75 g (3 oz) butter or margarine, cut
   into small pieces

75 g (3 oz) caster sugar
100 g (4 oz) semolina
50 g (2 oz) ground almonds
1 egg
few drops of almond essence
45–60 ml (3–4 tbsp) raspberry jam

■

GREASE a shallow 18 × 23 cm (7 × 9 inch) dish.

■

SPREAD the flaked almonds out on a large flat plate and microwave on
HIGH for 8–10 minutes until lightly browned, stirring once. Set aside to
cool.

■

MEANWHILE, make the pastry. Put the flour and salt into a bowl and rub in
the butter or margarine until the mixture resembles fine breadcrumbs. Add
30 ml (2 tbsp) cold water and bind to a smooth dough, adding a little extra
water if necessary.

■

ROLL out on a lightly floured surface and use to line the prepared dish.
Prick the pastry all over using a fork.

■

MICROWAVE on HIGH for 3–4 minutes or until the pastry looks slightly
dry all over. Leave to cool.

■

PUT the butter or margarine for the filling into a medium bowl and
microwave on HIGH for 1–1½ minutes or until melted. Stir in the sugar,
semolina, ground almonds, egg and almond essence and beat together.

■

SPREAD the jam over the base of the pastry case. Spoon the cake mixture on
top and sprinkle with the toasted almonds.

■

MICROWAVE on HIGH for 6–7 minutes until slightly risen and firm to the
touch. Leave to cool in the dish, then cut into sixteen slices before serving.

• Cream Slices •

Puff pastry is crisp and rises even higher in the microwave than when baked conventionally. The only disadvantage is the pale colour, but this can easily be disguised by icing.

MAKES 12

370 g (13 oz) packet ready-to-roll puff
  pastry, thawed
FOR THE FILLING
300 ml (½ pint) whipping cream
45 ml (4 level tbsp) strawberry jam

FOR THE ICING
double quantity Glacé icing (see
  page 86)
few drops red food colouring

CUT the pastry into four, then roll out each piece on a lightly floured surface to a rectangle measuring 18 × 25.5 cm (7 × 8 inches). Trim all of the edges to ensure that the pastry puffs during cooking. Prick the pastry all over with a fork.

PLACE one rectangle on a double thickness of absorbent kitchen paper on the turntable or the base of the cooker. Microwave on HIGH for 3 minutes until the pastry puffs up all over. Do not open the door during cooking or the pastry will collapse.

TRANSFER to a wire rack to cool. Repeat with the remaining pastry, using a clean piece of absorbent kitchen paper if the first piece becomes very moist.

WHEN all of the pastry is cool, trim the edges using a sharp knife and cut each piece into three crossways. Cut each piece in half horizontally.

WHIP the cream until it forms soft peaks then sandwich the pastry halves together with the jam and the cream.

MAKE the Glacé icing and transfer 30 ml (2 tbsp) of it to a small bowl or cup and colour it pink with a few drops of red food colouring. Spoon the pink icing into a greaseproof paper piping bag (see page 86).

SPREAD the remaining icing on top of the pastries. Snip the end off the piping bag and carefully pipe fine lines about 1 cm (½ inch) apart on top of the white Glacé icing.

DRAW a skewer or the point of a knife across the lines to make a feather pattern. Leave until set. These pastries are best eaten on the day of making.

• Jam or Lemon Curd Tarts •

It is important to prick the pastry thoroughly or it will puff up and lose its shape during cooking. Use half plain and half wholemeal flour to give the pastry some colour if you prefer.

MAKES 18

175 g (6 oz) plain flour
pinch of salt
75 g (3 oz) butter or block margarine

about 60 ml (4 level tbsp) jam or
  lemon curd

PUT the flour and salt into a bowl and rub in the butter or margarine until
the mixture resembles fine breadcrumbs. Stir in about 30 ml (2 tbsp) water
and mix to make a firm dough.

■

KNEAD lightly on a floured surface and roll out thinly. Using a 7.5 cm
(3 inch) fluted cutter cut out eighteen rounds. Line a microwave muffin tray
with six of the pastry rounds and prick thoroughly.

■

MICROWAVE on HIGH for 2 minutes or until the surface of the pastry looks
dry. Transfer the pastry cases to a wire rack and leave to cool. Repeat twice
with the remaining pastry rounds.

■

WHEN the cases are completely cold, fill with jam or lemon curd.

▪ FRESH FRUIT TARTLETS ▪

Take care when removing the pastry cases from the dishes as
they are very fragile.

MAKES 8

175 g (6 oz) plain flour
25 g (1 oz) plain wholemeal flour
25 g (1 oz) caster sugar
25 g (1 oz) ground toasted hazelnuts
pinch of salt
50 g (2 oz) butter or margarine
1 egg, beaten

FOR THE FILLING
double quantity Crème pâtissière (see
    page 90)
selection of prepared fresh fruit in
    season, such as strawberries,
    raspberries, cherries, kiwi fruit,
    grapes
FOR THE GLAZE
½ quantity Apricot glaze (see page 89)

PUT the flours, sugar, hazelnuts and salt into a bowl and mix together. Rub
in the butter or margarine until the mixture resembles fine breadcrumbs.
Make a well in the centre, add the egg and enough water to make a firm
dough.

■

TURN on to a lightly floured surface and knead for a few seconds until
smooth. Wrap in cling film and chill for 20–30 minutes until firm.

■

CUT the pastry in half, then roll out one half very thinly on a lightly floured
surface. Use to cover the base and sides of four inverted 10 cm (4 inch)
shallow glass flan dishes.

■

PRICK all over with a fork and microwave on HIGH, pastry side uppermost
for 2½–3 minutes or until the pastry is firm to the touch. Remove the pastry
cases from the dishes and invert on to a wire rack to cool. Repeat with the
remaining pastry to make eight pastry cases.

■

WHEN all the pastry cases are cool, fill with the Crème pâtissière and
decorate with the prepared fruit.

■

MAKE the glaze and carefully brush over the fruit. Serve as soon as possible.

Fun Cakes
for Children

There's nothing nicer than a home-made birthday cake,
and with the ones shown here there's the added bonus that
you don't even have to be good at cake icing.

• Funny Face Cakes •

Let your imagination loose on these cakes. If making them for
a party try making one face to look like each guest.

Makes about 24

100 g (4 oz) softened butter or soft tub
   margarine
100 g (4 oz) caster sugar
2 eggs
100 g (4 oz) self raising flour
30 ml (2 tbsp) milk

FOR THE ICING AND DECORATION
double quantity Glacé icing (see
   page 86)
chocolate vermicelli
assorted sweets such as sugar-coated
   chocolate beans, jelly sweets
    liquorice sweets
silver balls

PUT the butter or margarine, sugar, eggs, flour and milk into a bowl and beat
until smooth. Alternatively, put all the ingredients into a food processor or
mixer and mix until smooth.

ARRANGE six double layers of paper cases in a microwave muffin tray. Put a
heaped teaspoon of the cake mixture into each.

MICROWAVE on HIGH for 1–1½ minutes or until risen, but still look
slightly moist on the surface. Transfer to a wire rack and leave to cool.
Repeat three more times with the remaining mixture.

WHEN the cakes are cold, cover the tops completely with the icing. Use the
chocolate vermicelli to represent hair, and the sweets to represent eyes,
nose, ears and mouths to make funny faces. Leave to set.

· SWEETS CAKE ·

This cake is simple to make, but looks very pretty. Fill the
centre with your children's favourite sweets.

SERVES ABOUT 12

100 g (4 oz) softened butter or soft tub
  margarine
100 g (4 oz) caster sugar
100 g (4 oz) self raising flour
2.5 ml (½ level tsp) baking powder
2 eggs
about 30 ml (2 tbsp) milk
15 ml (1 level tbsp) cocoa powder
pink food colouring

FOR THE ICING AND DECORATION
150 g (5 oz) chocolate, broken into
  small pieces
100 g (4 oz) butter or margarine, cut
  into pieces
25.5 cm (10 inch) square cake board
½ quantity Glacé icing (see page 86)
assorted sweets
party streamers

GREASE a 1.6 litre (2¾ pint) ring mould and line the base with greaseproof
paper.

PUT the butter or margarine, sugar, flour, baking powder, eggs and 30 ml
(2 tbsp) milk into a bowl and beat until smooth. Alternatively, put all the
ingredients into a food processor or mixer and mix until smooth.

TRANSFER one third of the mixture into a separate bowl and sieve in the
cocoa powder. Beat until thoroughly mixed. Add a little extra milk if
necessary to make a soft dropping consistency.

TRANSFER half of the remaining mixture into another bowl and colour it
pink with a few drops of food colouring.

SPOON alternate spoonfuls of the three cake mixtures into the prepared
dish. Draw a knife through the mixture to make a marbled effect, then level
the surface.

STAND the ring mould on a roasting rack and microwave on HIGH for
4–5 minutes or until risen and firm to the touch, turning the cake during
cooking if rising unevenly. Leave to stand for 10 minutes, then turn out and
leave to cool on a wire rack.

WHEN the cake is cool, make the chocolate icing. Put the chocolate, butter
or margarine and 30 ml (2 tbsp) water in a small bowl and microwave on
LOW for 2–3 minutes. Stir until the chocolate and butter are melted. Leave
to cool until thick enough to coat the back of a spoon.

WHILE the icing is cooling trim the cake if necessary so that it stands flat,
then put it back on to the wire rack.

SPOON the icing over the top and sides of the cake using a palette knife to
help the icing coat the sides completely. Leave until set.

WHEN the chocolate icing is set, spoon the Glacé icing into a greaseproof
paper piping bag (see page 86) snip off the tip and pipe squiggles and dots on
the top of the cake. When set, place on cake board.

FILL the centre of the cake with sweets, tuck the ends of the streamers into
the sweets and let them trail out over the sides of the cake on to the table.

· SAND CASTLES ·

It is possible to cook all of these cakes at once, but cooking
four at a time improves the cakes, as they take less time to
cook and are, therefore, more moist. Although a lot of sugar
is used in this recipe (most is purely for display) if you prefer,
arrange the cakes on sand-coloured paper instead.

MAKES 8

*100 g (4 oz) softened butter or soft tub
    margarine
100 g (4 oz) caster sugar
2 eggs
100 g (4 oz) self raising flour*

*30 ml (2 tbsp) milk
30 ml (2 tbsp) apricot jam
175 g (6 oz) golden granulated sugar
cocktail sticks
coloured paper*

■

GREASE the bases of eight paper drinking cups.

■

PUT the butter or margarine, sugar, eggs, flour and milk into a bowl and beat
until smooth. Alternatively, put all the ingredients into a food processor or
mixer and mix until smooth.

■

DIVIDE the mixture evenly between the cups and arrange four in a circle on
the turntable or the base of the cooker.

■

MICROWAVE on HIGH for 1½–2 minutes until all the cakes are risen but still
look slightly moist on the surface. Turn out and leave to cool on a wire rack.

■

REPEAT with the remaining cakes.

■

PUT the jam and 10 ml (2 tbsp) water into a small heatproof bowl and
microwave on HIGH for 1 minute until melted. Stir well.

■

SPREAD the golden sugar out on a plate. Spear a cake on to a skewer or fork,
brush with the jam, then roll in the sugar to coat. Repeat with the remaining
cakes.

■

ARRANGE the cakes in a circle on a plate and sprinkle the remaining sugar
around the cakes to represent sand.

■

MAKE small flags from the coloured paper and attach them to the cocktail
sticks. Stick into the cakes.

▪ CALCULATOR CAKE ▪

If you find piping difficult, use an edible food colouring pen to
write the numerals on the calculator.

SERVES ABOUT 12–16

225 g (8 oz) softened butter or soft tub
   margarine
225 g (8 oz) caster sugar
225 g (8 oz) self raising flour
4 eggs
finely grated rind and juice of 1 lemon

FOR THE ICING AND DECORATION
1 quantity Lemon butter cream (see
   page 87)
three 220 g (8 oz) packets ready-to-roll
   fondant icing
yellow and black food colouring
½ quantity Glacé icing (see page 86)
silver balls

■

GREASE two 12.5 × 23 cm (5 × 9 inch) dishes and line the bases with
greaseproof paper.

■

PUT the butter or margarine, sugar, flour, eggs, lemon rind and juice into a
bowl and beat until smooth. Alternatively, put all the ingredients into a
food processor or mixer and mix until smooth.

■

DIVIDE the mixture between the two cake dishes. Stand one cake at a time
on a roasting rack and microwave on HIGH for 5–6 minutes. Leave to stand
for 10 minutes, then turn out and leave to cool on a wire rack.

■

COVER a baking tray or piece of card measuring about 23 × 30.5 cm
(9 × 12 inches) with foil or coloured paper.

■

SANDWICH the two cakes together with most of the butter cream and spread
a thin layer on the top and sides. Place on the baking tray or card.

■

COLOUR two packets of the icing yellow. Roll out thinly on a surface dusted
with icing sugar and use to cover the cake. Neaten the edges to make them
perfectly straight.

■

ROLL out the third packet of icing slightly more thickly and cut out a piece
measuring about 5 × 12 cm (2 × 5 inches). Brush with a little water and stick,
wet side down, onto the cake to represent the digital display.

■

USING a pastry cutter, cut out fourteen 2.5 cm (1 inch) circles from the
remaining icing. Brush with a little water and stick on to the cake to
represent the buttons. Cut a small rectangle to represent the on/off switch.

■

COLOUR the Glacé icing black and spoon into a greaseproof paper piping
bag (see page 86). Snip off the tip and pipe the numerals and mathematical
symbols on to the control buttons.

■

USING the silver balls write a message on the digital display.

• CLOCK CAKE •

This makes a very deep cake, so make sure that your cake dish
is at least 10 cm (4 inches) deep. Cover the dish with a piece of
greaseproof paper and then an upturned plate – the paper
prevents the plate sticking to the cake.

SERVES ABOUT 12

30 ml (2 tbsp) milk
100 g (4 oz) plain chocolate, broken
  into small pieces
225 g (8 oz) softened butter or soft tub
  margarine
225 g (8 oz) light soft brown sugar
225 g (8 oz) self raising flour
5 ml (1 level tsp) baking powder
4 eggs

FOR THE ICING AND DECORATION
1 quantity Chocolate butter cream (see
  page 87)
220 g (8 oz) packet ready-to-roll
  fondant icing
two 150 g (5 oz) packets chocolate
  finger biscuits
25.5 cm (10 inch) round cake board
ribbon

■

GREASE a deep 20.5 cm (8 inch) round dish and line the base with
greaseproof paper.

■

PUT the milk and the chocolate into a bowl and microwave on LOW for
4–5 minutes. Stir until the chocolate has melted.

■

PUT the butter or margarine, sugar, flour, baking powder and eggs into a
bowl and beat together until smooth. Alternatively, put all the ingredients
into a food processor or mixer and mix until smooth. Beat in the melted
chocolate.

■

POUR the mixture into the prepared dish and level the surface. Cover, then
stand on a roasting rack and microwave on MEDIUM for 12–13 minutes or
until risen and a skewer inserted in the centre comes out clean. Leave to
stand for 10 minutes, then turn out and leave to cool on a wire rack.

■

RESERVE 45 ml (3 tbsp) of the butter cream for piping. Spread a very thin
layer on top of the cake and the remainder around the sides.

■

PUT the cake on to the cake board. Roll out the fondant icing to a 20.5 cm
(8 inch) circle and place on top of the cake. Roll gently with a rolling pin to
ensure a flat surface.

■

CUT the chocolate biscuits to the depth of the cake and position around the
edge, using the butter cream to stick them on.

■

SPOON the reserved butter cream into a greaseproof paper piping bag (see
page 86), snip off the tip and pipe numerals and hands on to the clock face.
Tie the ribbon around the cake.

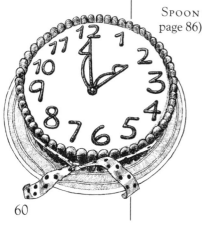

· ROBOT CAKE ·

This cake is very easy to make because it doesn't involve any piping – you don't even have to be particularly neat when covering with marzipan since the whole thing is covered in foil! Make sure that children remember to remove the foil before eating the cake.

SERVES ABOUT 20

350 g (12 oz) softened butter or soft
   tub margarine
350 g (12 oz) caster sugar
275 g (10 oz) self raising flour
50 g (2 oz) cocoa powder
10 ml (2 level tsp) baking powder
6 eggs
45 ml (3 tbsp) milk

FOR THE ICING AND DECORATION
60 ml (4 tbsp) apricot jam
three 250 g (9 oz) packets marzipan
icing sugar
liquorice laces
assorted sweets, such as jelly sweets
   and sugar-coated chocolate beans

GREASE two square 23 cm (9 inch) dishes and line the bases with greaseproof paper.

PUT the butter or margarine, sugar, flour, cocoa, baking powder, eggs and milk into a bowl and beat together until smooth. Alternatively, put all the ingredients into a food processor or mixer and mix until smooth.

DIVIDE the mixture between the prepared dishes and level the surfaces. Stand one cake at a time on a roasting rack and microwave on MEDIUM for 10–11 minutes or until risen, firm to the touch but still slightly moist on the surface. Leave to stand for 10 minutes, then turn out and cool on a wire rack.

WHEN the cakes are completely cold put them on a flat surface and, using a large sharp knife, trim the edges to make the cakes completely square.

CUT one of the cakes in half cross-ways, then cut one of the halves into quarters to make the arms and legs of the robot. Cut off the top third of the remaining half. The larger piece makes the robot's head.

COVER a large baking tray or piece of card measuring about 30.5 × 40.5 cm (12 × 16 inches) with foil or coloured paper.

PUT the apricot jam and 15 ml (1 tbsp) water into a small bowl and microwave on HIGH for 1 minute or until melted. Stir well.

PLACE the uncut cake in the middle of the cake board and brush the top and sides with the melted jam. Position the head at the top of the body pressing together to stick. Put the arms and legs in position. Brush the arms, legs and head with apricot jam.

ROLL out the marzipan thinly on a surface covered with icing sugar and use to coat the top and sides of the cake.

COVER the top and sides of the cake completely with a large piece of foil and smooth the surface so that you can see the shape of the cake. Cut out a square of the foil in the centre of the robots body to expose the marzipan.

PRESS liquorice laces and other sweets into the marzipan to represent the workings of the robot. Press two jelly sweets into the head to represent eyes. Using a permanent marker or felt pen draw a mouth on the foil.

• OWL CAKE •

Feathers, represented by overlapping brown and white
chocolate buttons, look quite realistic although they take time
to arrange. If you prefer, cover the cake with Chocolate butter
cream and simply mark with a fork to represent the feathers.

SERVES ABOUT 20

275 g (10 oz) softened butter or soft
tub margarine
275 g (10 oz) caster sugar
275 g (10 oz) self raising flour
10 ml (2 level tsp) baking powder
5 eggs
45 ml (3 tbsp) milk
few drops of vanilla essence

FOR THE ICING AND DECORATION
1½ quantities Chocolate butter cream
(see page 87)
three 51 g (2 oz) packets dark
chocolate buttons
two 51 g (2 oz) packets white
chocolate buttons
25 g (1 oz) flaked almonds
2 liquorice sweets
2 almonds with skins on
30.5 cm (12 inch) cake board

GREASE a 2.3 litre (4 pint) pudding basin and a 900 ml (1½ pint) pudding
basin and line the bases with greaseproof paper.

PUT the butter or margarine, sugar, flour, baking powder, eggs, milk and
vanilla essence into a bowl and beat together until smooth. Alternatively,
put all the ingredients into a food processor or mixer and mix until smooth.

SPOON into the prepared containers and level the surfaces. Cover the larger
cake, stand on a roasting rack and microwave on MEDIUM for
12–13 minutes until well risen and a skewer inserted in the centre comes
out clean. Leave to stand for 10 minutes, then turn out and leave to cool on
a wire rack.

COOK the remaining cake, as above on MEDIUM for 7–8 minutes until well
risen and a skewer inserted in the centre comes out clean. Leave to stand for
10 minutes, then turn out on to a wire rack and leave to cool.

WHEN the cakes are completely cool, cut a slice about 2.5 cm (1 inch) wide
from two sides of the large cake. Reserve the slices. Cut a slice from one side
of the small cake.

PLACE the cakes on the cake board, larger flat sides downwards, with the cut
side of the smaller cake against one of the cut sides of the larger cake. The
larger cake makes the owl's body and the smaller cake the owl's head.

COVER completely with butter cream. Cover the slices cut from the large
cake with butter cream and position one on each side of the body to
resemble wings.

ARRANGE the chocolate buttons on the cake in overlapping rows to
represent feathers, leaving the chest and face clear.

ARRANGE the flaked almonds on the chest to represent feathers. Smooth the
face, then use liquorice sweets and one flaked almond to represent the eyes
and beak. Use two whole almonds to represent the ears.

IF liked, wind streamers around the liquorice sweets to make the eyes look
bigger.

· DOUBLE DECKER BUS CAKE ·

Use dark red food colouring to get the most authentic colour.
To make the cake very personal, cut out small photographs
and stick them at the windows.

SERVES ABOUT 15 TO 20

*275 g (10 oz) softened butter or soft
  tub margarine*
275 g (10 oz) self raising flour
225 g (8 oz) caster sugar
5 ml (1 level tsp) baking powder
150 g (5 oz) ground rice
4 eggs
45 ml (3 tbsp) milk

60 ml (4 tbsp) strawberry jam
FOR THE ICING AND DECORATION
*four 220 g (8 oz) packets ready-to-roll
  fondant icing*
red and black food colouring
1 quantity Glacé icing (see page 86)
4 liquorice Catherine wheels
25.5 cm (10 inch) square cake board

GREASE a 1.7 litre (3 pint) loaf dish and line the base with greaseproof paper.

■

PUT the butter or margarine, flour, sugar, baking powder, ground rice, eggs
and milk into a bowl and beat until smooth. Alternatively, put all the
ingredients into a food processor or mixer and mix until smooth.

■

POUR half of the cake mixture into the prepared loaf dish and level the
surface. Stand on a roasting rack and microwave on HIGH for 5–6 minutes
until well risen and a skewer inserted into the centre comes out clean. Turn
the cake once during cooking if rising unevenly. Leave to stand for
5 minutes, then turn out and leave to cool on a wire rack.

■

WASH and dry the loaf dish and lightly grease. Re-line the base with
greaseproof paper. Pour the remaining cake mixture into the dish and cook
as above. Leave to stand for 5 minutes, then turn out and leave to cool on a
wire rack.

■

WHEN the cakes are completely cool, sandwich them together with 45 ml
(3 tbsp) of the strawberry jam and place on the cake board. Put the
remaining jam in a bowl with 10 ml (2 tsp) water and microwave on HIGH
for 30 seconds or until melted. Brush all over the cake.

■

COLOUR three packets of the icing red. Roll out on a surface dusted with
icing sugar and use to cover the cake. Neaten the edges.

■

ROLL out the remaining icing and cut out the windows, doors and
headlights of the bus. Brush with a little water and stick on to the bus.

■

COLOUR the Glacé icing black and spoon into a greaseproof paper piping
bag (see page 86). Snip off the tip and pipe the window frames, the number
of the bus and faces looking through the windows.

■

USE the Catherine wheels to represent the wheels of the bus.

BREADS, TEABREADS AND SCONES

There are few things as homely and welcoming as a tea-tray stacked with home-made breads, teabreads, scones and cakes. Even beginners will have perfect results with the following recipes.

• GRANARY BREAD •

Use your microwave to speed up the rising process (see Quick Tips page 10).

MAKES ONE 450 G (1 LB) LOAF

450 g (1 lb) granary flour
5 ml (1 level tsp) salt

25 g (1 oz) butter or margarine
one sachet easy blend yeast

■

GREASE a 1.7 litre (3 pint) loaf dish.

■

PUT the flour and salt into a large bowl and rub in the butter or margarine. Stir in the yeast.

■

PUT 300 ml ($\frac{1}{2}$ pint) water into a jug and microwave on HIGH for 1–2 minutes. Pour on to the flour and mix to form a soft dough.

■

TURN out on to a lightly floured surface and knead for 10 minutes or until the dough is smooth and no longer sticky. Place in a large bowl, cover with a clean tea-towel and leave to rise in a warm place for about 1 hour until doubled in size.

■

TURN the dough out on to a lightly floured surface and knead lightly until smooth. Shape the dough to fit the loaf dish, place in the dish and cover with a clean tea-towel. Leave to prove for about 30 minutes until the dough reaches the top of the dish.

■

UNCOVER, stand on a roasting rack and microwave on HIGH for about 6 minutes or until risen and firm to the touch. Leave to stand for 10 minutes before turning out on to a wire rack to cool. If liked, place under a hot grill to brown.

Griddle Scones (page 75), Welsh Cakes (page 73), Wholemeal Bread (page 66)

· RYE BREAD ·

Rye flour gives bread colour and flavour, but it needs to be
mixed with strong flour as it produces dense, heavy bread if
used on its own.

MAKES ONE 450 G (1 LB) LOAF

150 g (5 oz) rye flour
150 g (5 oz) strong white flour
5 ml (1 level tsp) salt
5 ml (1 level tsp) caraway or fennel
  seeds

one sachet easy blend yeast
90 ml (6 tbsp) milk
15 ml (1 tbsp) black treacle

■

GREASE a 1.7 litre (3 pint) loaf dish.

■

PUT the flours and salt into a large bowl. Stir in the caraway or fennel seeds
and yeast.

■

PUT 90 ml (6 tbsp) water, the milk and the treacle into a jug and microwave
on HIGH for about 1 minute or until just warm. Pour on to the flour and
mix to form a firm dough.

■

TURN the dough out on to a lightly floured surface and knead for
10 minutes or until smooth and no longer sticky. Place in a large bowl, cover
with a clean tea-towel and leave to rise in a warm place for about 1 hour
until doubled in size.

■

TURN the dough out on to a lightly floured surface and knead lightly until
smooth. Shape the dough to fit the dish, place in the dish and cover with a
clean tea-towel. Leave to prove for about 30 minutes until the dough reaches
the top of the dish.

■

UNCOVER, stand on a roasting rack and microwave on HIGH for about
6–8 minutes or until well-risen and firm to the touch. Leave to stand for
10 minutes, then turn out and leave to cool on a wire rack.

Marbled Apricot and Sesame Seed Teabread (page 72),
Malted Fruit Loaf (page 68), Chocolate, Date and Nut
Loaf (page 69)

· WHOLEMEAL BREAD AND ROLLS ·

This bread will not have the characteristic crisp crust of conventionally baked bread, because when bread is cooked in the microwave moisture is drawn to the surface and prevents it from becoming crisp. However, this can easily be overcome by browning the loaves under a hot grill after cooking.

MAKES TWO 450 G (1 LB) LOAVES OR 16 ROLLS

275 g (10 oz) strong wholemeal flour
275 g (10 oz) strong white flour
10 ml (2 level tsp) salt
25 g (1 oz) butter or margarine

15 ml (1 level tbsp) caster sugar
one sachet easy blend yeast
milk, to glaze
15 ml (1 level tbsp) poppy seeds

∎

To make loaves
GREASE two 1.7 litre (3 pint) loaf dishes.

∎

PUT the flours and salt into a large bowl. Rub in the butter or margarine and stir in the sugar and yeast.

∎

PUT 450 ml (¾ pint) water into jug and microwave on HIGH for 1–2 minutes or until just warm. Pour on to the flour and mix to form a soft dough.

∎

TURN out on to a lightly floured surface and knead for 10 minutes or until the dough is smooth and no longer sticky. Place in a large bowl, cover with a clean tea-towel and leave to rise in a warm place for about 1 hour until doubled in size.

∎

TURN the dough out on to a lightly floured surface and knead lightly until smooth. Divide the dough in two and shape each piece to fit the dishes. Cover the dishes with a clean tea-towel and leave to prove for about 30 minutes until the dough reaches the top of the dish.

∎

UNCOVER, brush with milk and sprinkle with poppy seeds. Stand on a roasting rack and microwave one loaf at a time on HIGH for 6 minutes or until risen and firm to the touch. Leave to stand in the dish for 10 minutes, then turn out and leave to cool on a wire rack. If liked, place the loaves under a hot grill to brown.

∎

To make rolls
GREASE two shallow 20.5 cm (8 inch) cake dishes.

∎

FOLLOW the recipe as far as step 5 and divide the dough into sixteen equal pieces. Shape each piece into a smooth ball. Place one ball in the centre of each prepared dish and place seven balls around the central ball. Cover the dishes with a clean tea-towel and leave to rise in a warm place until doubled in size.

∎

UNCOVER, brush with milk and sprinkle with the poppy seeds. Stand on a roasting rack and microwave one dish at a time on HIGH for 6 minutes until well risen and firm to the touch. Leave to stand in the dishes for 10 minutes, then turn out and leave to cool on a wire rack. If liked, place under a hot grill to brown. Pull the rolls apart, to serve.

▪ IRISH SODA BREAD ▪

This works very well in the microwave and like
conventionally baked soda bread, it is best eaten straight from
the cooker.

MAKES ONE 450 G (1 LB) LOAF

450 g (1 lb) plain wholemeal flour,
  plus extra for sifting
5 ml (1 level tsp) salt
5 ml (1 level tsp) bicarbonate of soda

15 g (½ oz) butter or margarine
10 ml (2 level tsp) cream of tartar
5 ml (1 level tsp) dark soft brown
  sugar
about 300 ml (½ pint) milk

■

GREASE a microwave baking tray or a large flat plate. Mix the flour, salt and
bicarbonate of soda in a large bowl and rub in the butter or margarine until
the mixture resembles fine breadcrumbs.

■

ADD the cream of tartar and sugar to the milk and stir until dissolved. Add
to the flour mixture and mix to form a soft dough, adding a little more milk
if necessary.

■

KNEAD the dough on a lightly floured surface until it is firm and smooth and
there are no cracks.

■

FLATTEN out the dough to a round about 18 cm (7 inches) in diameter and
place it on the prepared tray or plate.

■

BRUSH the surface of the dough with a little milk and mark a deep cross on
the top with a knife. Sift a little flour on top.

■

STAND on a roasting rack and microwave on HIGH for 8–9 minutes or until
the bread is well risen and the surface looks dry, turning the dish two or
three times during cooking. Turn the bread over and microwave on HIGH
for a further 1–1½ minutes or until the bottom looks dry. Leave to stand for
2–3 minutes, then serve immediately. This bread is best served warm.

· MALTED FRUIT LOAF ·

If using a food processor to mix, use the plastic blade to avoid
chopping the sultanas.

MAKES ONE 450 G (1 LB) LOAF

450 g (1 lb) strong white flour
5 ml (1 level tsp) salt
one sachet easy blend yeast
225 g (8 oz) sultanas

45 ml (3 tbsp) malt extract
30 ml (2 tbsp) black treacle
25 g (1 oz) butter or margarine

■

GREASE a 1.7 litre (3 pint) loaf dish.

■

PUT the flour and salt into a large bowl and stir in the yeast and sultanas.

■

PUT the malt extract, treacle and butter or margarine into a medium bowl
with 450 ml ($\frac{3}{4}$ pint) water and microwave on HIGH for 1–2 minutes or until
melted. Stir into the dry ingredients and beat well for 5 minutes.
Alternatively, put the dry ingredients into a food processor or mixer, add
the melted ingredients and beat for 3 minutes.

■

POUR the batter into the prepared dish, cover with a clean tea-towel and
leave to rise in a warm place for about 45 minutes until doubled in size.

■

UNCOVER, stand on a roasting rack and microwave on HIGH for 6 minutes
or until well-risen and firm to the touch. Leave to stand for 10 minutes, then
turn out on to a wire rack to cool. If liked, place the loaf under a hot grill to
brown.

· APPLE, DATE AND FIG TEABREAD ·

The apple and dried fruit keeps this teabread moist and sweet,
so little extra sugar is needed.

MAKES 16 SLICES

225 g (8 oz) cooking apples, peeled,
  cored and chopped
75 g (3 oz) dried stoned dates,
  chopped
75 g (3 oz) dried figs, chopped
100 g (4 oz) softened butter or soft tub
  margarine

45 ml (3 tbsp) golden syrup
30 ml (2 tbsp) milk
225 g (8 oz) plain wholemeal flour
7.5 ml (1$\frac{1}{2}$ level tsp) baking powder
finely grated rind of 1 lemon
2 eggs

■

GREASE a 1.7 litre (3 pint) loaf dish and line the base with greaseproof paper.

■

PUT the apples, dates, figs and 15 ml (1 tbsp) water in a bowl. Cover and
microwave on HIGH for 4–5 minutes until the apple is tender, stirring once.

■

STIR in the butter or margarine and the syrup and mix until the fat is
melted. Stir in the remaining ingredients and beat thoroughly together.
Spoon into the dish and level the surface.

■

STAND on a roasting rack and microwave on HIGH for 7–8 minutes until risen and firm to the touch, turning the dish two or three times if rising unevenly. Leave to stand for 10 minutes, then turn out and leave to cool on a wire rack. Serve cut into slices.

▪ CHOCOLATE, DATE AND NUT LOAF ▪

This loaf tends to rise unevenly, so watch it carefully and give the dish an occasional quarter turn during cooking.

MAKES 16 SLICES

75 g (3 oz) dried stoned dates, chopped
75 g (3 oz) plain chocolate
25 g (1 oz) butter or margarine
150 g (5 oz) plain flour
25 g (1 oz) caster sugar

2.5 ml (½ level tsp) baking powder
2.5 ml (½ level tsp) bicarbonate of soda
1 egg, beaten
75 g (3 oz) walnuts, chopped
100 ml (4 fl oz) milk

▪

GREASE a 1.7 litre (3 pint) loaf dish and line the base with greaseproof paper. Put the dates, chocolate, butter or margarine and 100 ml (4 fl oz) water in a medium bowl, and microwave on LOW for 5 minutes until the chocolate has melted, stirring once.

▪

STIR in the remaining ingredients and beat thoroughly together to make a soft dropping consistency. Spoon the mixture into the prepared dish and smooth the top.

▪

STAND on a roasting rack and microwave on HIGH for 6 minutes until the cake is well risen and firm to the touch, but still looks slightly moist on the surface. Turn the dish two or three times during cooking if rising unevenly.

▪

LEAVE the cake to stand in the dish for 10 minutes, then carefully turn out and leave to cool on a wire rack. Serve sliced.

• BANANA TEABREAD •

Mashed banana stirred into almost any cake mixture ensures
that it remains moist.

MAKES 8 SLICES

225 g (8 oz) plain wholemeal flour
10 ml (2 level tsp) ground cinnamon
5 ml (1 level tsp) ground mixed spice
100 g (4 oz) butter or margarine

100 g (4 oz) light soft brown sugar
2 eggs
2 ripe bananas, peeled and mashed,
  about 225 g (8 oz) prepared weight

GREASE a 1.7 litre (3 pint) loaf dish and line the base with greaseproof paper.

PUT all the ingredients into a bowl and beat well with a wooden spoon until
evenly mixed. Alternatively, put all the ingredients into a food processor
and blend until smooth. Spoon into the loaf dish and smooth the top.

STAND on a roasting rack and microwave on MEDIUM for 6 minutes until
firm to the touch. Leave to cool in the dish. Serve, cut into slices.

• BRAN TEABREAD •

Do not use flaked bran breakfast cereal for this recipe as it
does not disintegrate after soaking.

MAKES 16 SLICES

100 g (4 oz) bran breakfast cereal (not
  flaked)
75 g (3 oz) dark soft brown sugar
225 g (8 oz) mixed dried fruit
50 g (2 oz) mixed chopped nuts

300 ml (½ pint) milk
100 g (4 oz) self raising flour
5 ml (1 level tsp) ground mixed spice
1 egg, beaten

GREASE a 1.7 litre (3 pint) loaf dish and line the base with greaseproof paper.

PUT the bran cereal, sugar, fruit and nuts into a medium bowl. Pour over
the milk and microwave on HIGH for 3 minutes or until most of the liquid
has been absorbed.

STIR in the flour, spice and egg, and beat thoroughly together. Spoon the
mixture into the prepared dish and level the surface.

STAND on a roasting rack and microwave on HIGH for 7–8 minutes or until
risen and firm to the touch.

LEAVE to stand for 10 minutes, then turn out to cool on a wire rack. Serve
sliced and buttered.

· PRUNE AND WALNUT TEABREAD ·

This wholesome teabread is sweetened just with chopped prunes.

MAKES 14 SLICES

225 g (8 oz) self raising wholemeal flour
5 ml (1 level tsp) mixed ground spice
25 g (1 oz) softened butter or soft tub margarine
300 ml (½ pint) milk

1 egg, beaten
100 g (4 oz) prunes, stoned and chopped
50 g (2 oz) walnut halves, chopped
a few walnut halves, to decorate

GREASE a 1.7 litre (3 pint) loaf dish and line the base with greaseproof paper.

PUT the flour, spice, butter or margarine, milk and egg into a bowl and beat until smooth. Alternatively, put all the ingredients into a food processor or mixer and mix until smooth.

SPOON half of the batter into the prepared dish. Sprinkle the chopped prunes and walnuts evenly over the batter. Spoon the remaining batter over the top and level the surface. Press the walnut halves along the top to decorate.

STAND on a roasting rack and microwave on HIGH for 7–8 minutes until well risen and firm to the touch, turning the dish two or three times if rising unevenly.

LEAVE to stand for 10 minutes, then turn out to cool on a wire rack. Serve cut into slices.

· MARBLED APRICOT AND SESAME SEED TEABREAD ·

For a good marbled effect, use a teaspoon to spoon the mixture into the dish.

MAKES 16 SLICES

225 g (8 oz) no-soak dried apricots
100 g (4 oz) plain flour
100 g (4 oz) plain wholemeal flour
5 ml (1 level tsp) baking powder
100 g (4 oz) softened butter or soft tub margarine

50 g (2 oz) caster sugar
2 eggs
90 ml (6 tbsp) milk
25 g (1 oz) sesame seeds
toasted sesame seeds, to decorate

■

GREASE a 1.7 litre (3 pint) loaf dish and line the base with greaseproof paper.

■

PUT the apricots and 150 ml (¼ pint) water into a bowl. Cover and microwave on HIGH for 4–5 minutes until the apricots are softened, stirring occasionally. Cool slightly, then purée in a blender or food processor.

■

PUT the flours, baking powder, butter or margarine, sugar, eggs and milk into a bowl and beat until smooth. Alternatively, put all of the ingredients into a food processor or mixer and mix until smooth. Stir in the sesame seeds.

■

PUT alternate spoonfuls of the apricot purée and the cake mixture into the prepared dish. Level the surface and sprinkle with toasted sesame seeds.

■

STAND on a roasting rack and microwave on HIGH for 8–9 minutes until risen and firm to the touch, turning the dish two or three times if rising unevenly. Leave to cool in the dish, then turn out and serve sliced.

ᐧ WELSH CAKES ᐧ

Although these tea-cakes should be eaten immediately, they
can be reheated successfully from cold if wrapped in
absorbent kitchen paper, and microwaved on HIGH for
1–2 minutes.

MAKES 12

225 g (8 oz) plain flour
5 ml (1 level tsp) baking powder
pinch of salt
50 g (2 oz) butter or margarine
50 g (2 oz) lard

75 g (3 oz) caster sugar
50 g (2 oz) currants
1 egg, beaten
about 30 ml (2 tbsp) milk

■

HEAT a large browning dish, skillet or griddle on HIGH for 4–5 minutes.
Do not allow the dish to become too hot or the cakes will burn.

■

SIFT the flour, baking powder and salt into a bowl. Rub in the butter or
margarine and lard until the mixture resembles fine breadcrumbs, then stir
in the sugar and currants. Add the egg and enough milk to bind the mixture
together to form a soft dough.

■

TURN out on to a lightly floured surface and roll out to 0.5 cm (¼ inch)
thickness. Using a 7.5 cm (3 inch) plain cutter, cut out twelve cakes, re-
rolling as necessary.

■

QUICKLY place six cakes on to the browning dish and microwave on HIGH
for 1½ minutes. Turn them over and microwave on HIGH for a further
1½ minutes. Serve whilst still hot.

■

REPEAT with the remaining cakes, heating the browning dish for
2 minutes before cooking the second batch.

▪ WHOLEMEAL YOGURT SCONES ▪

These scones can be reheated in the same way as Welsh cakes
(see page 73).

MAKES 10

50 g (2 oz) currants or raisins
75 g (3 oz) plain flour
150 g (5 oz) plain wholemeal flour
15 ml (1 level tbsp) baking powder
pinch of nutmeg

50 g (2 oz) butter or margarine
50 g (2 oz) light soft brown sugar
150 ml (¼ pint) natural yogurt
about 45 ml (3 tbsp) milk

▪

COAT the currants or raisins in 25 g (1 oz) plain flour. Sift the remaining
plain and wholemeal flour into a bowl with the baking powder and nutmeg.

▪

RUB in the butter or margarine until the mixture resembles fine
breadcrumbs then stir in the sugar and currants or raisins.

▪

MAKE a well in the centre, then pour in the yogurt and milk. Mix with a
palette knife to make a soft dough, adding a little extra milk if necessary.
Leave to stand for about 5 minutes to allow the bran in the flour to absorb
the liquid. Knead the dough lightly on a floured surface until just smooth.

▪

HEAT a large browning dish, skillet or griddle on HIGH for 4–5 minutes.
Do not allow the dish to become too hot or the scones will burn. If
necessary, allow the dish to cool slightly.

▪

ROLL out the dough to a 2 cm (¾ inch) thickness, then using a 5 cm (2 inch)
round cutter, cut out ten scones, re-rolling the dough as necessary.

▪

QUICKLY place five scones on the browning dish and microwave on HIGH
for 2 minutes. Turn the scones over and microwave on HIGH for a further
2 minutes. Reheat the browning dish on HIGH for 2 minutes, then repeat
with the remaining scones. Eat while still hot, spread with butter.

· GRIDDLE SCONES ·

A microwave browning dish, skillet or griddle gives perfectly
browned scones just like a conventional griddle.

MAKES 8

225 g (8 oz) white self raising flour
2.5 ml (½ level tsp) salt
15 g (½ oz) butter or margarine

25 g (1 oz) caster sugar
about 150 ml (¼ pint) milk or
buttermilk

■

HEAT a large browning dish, skillet or griddle on HIGH for 4–5 minutes.
Do not allow the dish to become too hot or the scones will burn. If
necessary, allow the dish to cool slightly.

■

SIFT the flour and salt into a bowl. Rub in the butter or margarine, then stir in
the sugar. Add enough milk or buttermilk to give a soft but manageable dough.

■

KNEAD lightly on a floured surface, divide in two and roll into two rounds
0.5 cm (¼ inch) thick. Cut each round into four.

■

QUICKLY place four quarters on the browning dish and microwave on
HIGH for 1½ minutes. Turn the scones over and microwave on HIGH for a
further 2 minutes. Repeat with the remaining scones, without reheating the
browning dish. Eat while still hot, spread with butter.

· BRAN MUFFINS ·

The perfect quick breakfast – weigh out the dry ingredients
the night before and then add the liquid in the morning.

MAKES 8

50 g (2 oz) bran
75 g (3 oz) plain wholemeal flour
7.5 ml (1½ level tsp) baking powder

1 egg, beaten
300 ml (½ pint) milk
30 ml (2 tbsp) clear honey

■

PUT the bran, flour and baking powder in a bowl and mix together. Add the
egg, milk and honey and stir until well mixed.

■

DIVIDE the mixture between an eight-hole microwave muffin tray.
Microwave on HIGH for 5–6 minutes until firm to the touch.

■

LEAVE to stand for 5 minutes. Split each muffin in half horizontally and
serve while still warm, spread with butter or margarine.

· CHELSEA BUNS ·

A honey glaze browned under the grill disguises the pale crust
of these buns.

MAKES 8

275 g (10 oz) strong white flour
pinch of salt
15 g (½ oz) butter or margarine
one sachet easy blend yeast
200 ml (7 fl oz) milk
1 egg, beaten

FOR THE FILLING
50 g (2 oz) butter
75 g (3 oz) mixed dried fruit
25 g (1 oz) chopped mixed peel
50 g (2 oz) light soft brown sugar
1.25 ml (¼ level tsp) mixed spice
FOR THE GLAZE
30 ml (2 tbsp) clear honey

■

GREASE a shallow, loose-bottomed 20.5 cm (8 inch) round dish.

■

PUT the flour and salt into a bowl and rub in the butter or margarine. Stir in
the yeast.

■

PUT the milk into a jug and microwave on HIGH for 1–2 minutes or until
just warm. Pour on to the flour, add the egg and mix together to form a soft
dough.

■

TURN out on to a lightly floured surface and knead for about 10 minutes or
until smooth and no longer sticky. Place in large bowl, cover with a clean
tea-towel and leave to rise in a warm place for about 1 hour until doubled in
size.

■

TURN the dough out on to a lightly floured surface and knead until smooth.
Roll out to a rectangle 30.5 × 23 cm (12 × 9 inches).

■

PLACE the butter for the filling in a small bowl and microwave on HIGH for
1 minute or until melted. Brush the dough with melted butter and sprinkle
with the fruit, peel, brown sugar and spice.

■

ROLL up from the longest edge like a Swiss roll and seal the edge with water.
Cut into eight equal slices and place these, cut side down, in the prepared
dish. Cover with a clean tea-towel and leave to rise until the slices fill the
dish.

■

UNCOVER, stand on a roasting rack and microwave on HIGH for 6 minutes
until well risen and firm to the touch. Allow to stand for 10 minutes before
turning out of the dish. Brush with the honey and brown under a hot grill.
Allow to cool on a wire rack before serving.

BISCUITS

Home-made biscuits taste much better that bought ones and they are remarkably easy to make. Perfect with tea and coffee, they also make ideal gifts.

▪ FLAPJACKS ▪

These are one of the quickest and easiest biscuits to make in the microwave.

MAKES 16

75 g (3 oz) butter or margarine
50 g (2 oz) light soft brown sugar

30 ml (2 tbsp) golden syrup
175 g (6 oz) porridge oats

GREASE a shallow 12.5 × 23 cm (5 × 9 inch) dish.

■

PUT the butter or margarine, sugar and syrup into a large bowl. Microwave on HIGH for 2 minutes until the sugar has dissolved, stirring once. Stir well then mix in the oats.

■

PRESS the mixture into the dish. Stand on a roasting rack and microwave on HIGH for 2–3 minutes until firm to the touch.

■

LEAVE to cool slightly, then mark into sixteen bars. Allow to cool completely before turning out of the dish.

· DATE AND WALNUT BARS ·

This mixture will start to cook around the edges first – it is
cooked when the mixture in the centre bubbles as vigorously
as the mixture around the edge of the dish.

MAKES 12

225 g (8 oz) stoned dates, finely
   chopped
30 ml (2 tbsp) clear honey
100 g (4 oz) wholemeal flour
175 g (6 oz) butter or margarine, cut

   into small pieces
50 g (2 oz) dark soft brown sugar
100 g (4 oz) porridge oats
50 g (2 oz) walnuts, finely chopped

■

PUT the dates, honey and 150 ml (¼ pint) water into a medium bowl, and
microwave on HIGH for 3–5 minutes until the dates are very soft and the
mixture has thickened.

■

PUT the flour into a bowl and rub in the butter or margarine until the
mixture resembles fine breadcrumbs. Stir in the sugar, oats and walnuts.

■

PRESS half of the mixture into the base of a shallow 23 cm (9 inch) square
dish. Microwave on HIGH for 4 minutes until the mixture just bubbles all
over the surface.

■

SPOON the dates evenly over the cooked mixture and sprinkle with the
remaining oat mixture. Microwave on HIGH for 3 minutes.

■

MARK into twelve bars while warm and leave to cool in the dish. When
cold, turn out and cut through into bars.

· CHOCOLATE-MINT
BISCUITS ·

Biscuits should always be cooked in a circle, spaced well apart
to allow for the spreading mixture.

MAKES 24

200 g (7 oz) plain wholemeal flour
45 ml (3 level tbsp) cocoa powder
100 g (4 oz) butter or margarine

100 g (4 oz) light soft brown sugar
1 egg, beaten
1.25 ml (¼ tsp) peppermint flavouring

■

SIFT the flour and cocoa powder into a bowl and add any bran remaining in
the sieve. Rub in the butter or margarine until the mixture resembles fine
breadcrumbs, then stir in the sugar. Add the egg and peppermint flavouring
and mix to form a dough.

■

SHAPE the dough into twenty-four walnut-sized balls. Arrange eight in a
circle around the edge of a baking tray or large flat plate and flatten slightly
with a fork.

■

MICROWAVE on HIGH for 2½–3 minutes until the surface of the biscuits
looks dry. Carefully transfer to a wire rack, then repeat with the remaining
balls in batches of eight.

• CARROT BISCUITS •

The grated carrot gives these biscuits a nice moist texture and
an interesting colour.

MAKES 24

75 g (3 oz) butter or margarine
75 g (3 oz) light soft brown sugar
60 ml (4 tbsp) clear honey
1 egg, beaten
100 g (4 oz) carrots, scrubbed and
grated

175 g (6 oz) self raising wholemeal
flour
5 ml (1 level tsp) baking powder
100 g (4 oz) porridge oats
25 g (1 oz) sesame seeds
50 g (2 oz) raisins

■

PUT the butter or margarine, sugar and honey into a large bowl and
microwave on HIGH for 1–2 minutes until hot. Stir until the butter or
margarine has melted and the sugar dissolved.

■

ADD the egg, carrots, flour, baking powder, oats, sesame seeds and raisins
and mix well.

■

PLACE six heaped dessertspoonfuls of the mixture in a circle on a microwave
baking tray.

■

MICROWAVE on MEDIUM for 4–5 minutes until the surface of the biscuits
looks dry. Transfer to a wire rack to cool. Repeat three times with the
remaining mixture to make twenty-four biscuits.

• JUMBLES •

These biscuits are very pale in colour – as they would be if
made conventionally.

MAKES 20

150 g (5 oz) softened butter or soft tub
margarine
150 g (5 oz) caster sugar
1 egg, beaten

275 g (10 oz) self raising flour
5 ml (1 level tsp) grated lemon rind
50 g (2 oz) ground almonds
20 whole blanched almonds

■

PUT the butter or margarine and sugar into a large bowl and beat together
until they are pale and fluffy.

■

BEAT half of the egg into the creamed mixture, then mix in the flour, lemon
rind, ground almonds and remaining egg.

■

FORM into twenty walnut-sized balls and place eight in a circle on a
microwave baking tray, spacing them well apart. Press out with a fork to a
thickness of about 0.5 cm ($\frac{1}{4}$ inch). Press an almond on top of each biscuit.

■

MICROWAVE on HIGH for 1–2 minutes until the surface of the biscuits
looks dry.

■

ALLOW the Jumbles to stand for 1 minute, then transfer to a wire rack to
cool. Repeat with the remaining balls.

• PEANUT BUTTER BISCUITS •

Crunchy peanut butter gives these biscuits a good texture, but
the smooth variety can be used – the flavour will not be
affected.

MAKES 16

60 ml (4 level tbsp) crunchy peanut
    butter
75 g (3 oz) dark soft brown sugar
50 g (2 oz) softened butter or soft tub
    margarine

1 egg
100 g (4 oz) self raising wholemeal
    flour

■

PUT the peanut butter, sugar and butter or margarine into a large bowl and
beat together until they are very soft and fluffy. Beat in the egg, then stir in
the flour to make a firm dough.

■

SHAPE the dough into sixteen walnut-sized smooth balls. Place eight in a
circle on a microwave baking tray, spacing them well apart.

■

PRESS criss-cross lines on each ball of dough with a fork to flatten slightly.

■

MICROWAVE on HIGH for 2 minutes until the surface of the biscuits looks
dry. Allow the biscuits to cool slightly on the baking tray, then transfer
them to a wire rack to cool completely. Repeat with the remaining balls.

• MUESLI BISCUITS •

Use sugar-free muesli otherwise the biscuits will be very
sweet.

MAKES 16

100 g (4 oz) softened butter or soft tub
    margarine
50 g (2 oz) demerara sugar
15 ml (1 tbsp) clear honey

50 g (2 oz) self raising wholemeal
    flour
200 g (7 oz) muesli
50 g (2 oz) dried apricots, finely
    chopped
1 egg yolk

■

PUT the butter or margarine and sugar into a large bowl and beat together
until pale and fluffy. Add the honey, flour, muesli, apricots and egg yolk and
mix well together to form a firm dough.

■

SHAPE the dough into sixteen smooth walnut-sized balls. Place eight in a
circle on a microwave baking tray, spacing them well apart.

■

MICROWAVE on HIGH for 2 minutes. Allow the biscuits to cool slightly,
then transfer them to a wire rack to cool completely. Repeat with the
remaining balls.

Peanut Butter Biscuits (above), *Jumbles* (page 79),
Date and Walnut Bars (page 78)

· CHOCOLATE NUT BARS ·

Both chewy and crunchy at the same time, these delicious
chocolate bars are a perfect teatime filler.

MAKES 16

100 g (4 oz) self raising flour
90 ml (6 level tbsp) porridge oats
100 g (4 oz) softened butter or soft tub
   margarine
50 g (2 oz) caster sugar
50 g (2 oz) dark soft brown sugar

1.25 ml ($\frac{1}{4}$ level tsp) salt
2.5 ml ($\frac{1}{2}$ tsp) vanilla flavouring
1 egg
75 g (3 oz) plain chocolate, broken
   into small pieces
50 g (2 oz) chopped mixed nuts

■

GREASE a shallow 23 × 18 cm (9 × 7 inch) dish.

■

PUT the flour into a large bowl and mix in the oats.

■

PUT the butter or margarine, sugars, salt, vanilla flavouring and egg into a
large bowl and beat together until they are pale and fluffy. Add the flour and
oats and thoroughly mix the ingredients together.

■

SPREAD the mixture in the prepared dish and smooth the top. Microwave
on HIGH for 4–5 minutes until risen, but still looks slightly moist on the
surface.

■

ALLOW the cake to stand in the dish for 3–5 minutes, then turn out on to a
wire rack to cool.

■

PUT the chocolate into a small bowl. Microwave on LOW for 3 minutes
until the chocolate becomes soft and glossy on top. Stir until smooth.

■

SPREAD the melted chocolate over the cooled cake and sprinkle it with the
nuts. Cut the cake into sixteen bars just before the chocolate sets.

· CHOCOLATE FUDGE
COOKIES ·

These simple biscuits are fun for children to make.

MAKES 24

100 g (4 oz) softened butter or soft tub
   margarine
75 g (3 oz) light soft brown sugar

175 g (6 oz) plain flour
30 ml (2 level tbsp) cocoa powder

■

PUT the butter or margarine and sugar into a large bowl and beat together
until pale and fluffy. Sift in the flour and cocoa and stir together to make a
smooth dough.

■

SHAPE the dough into twenty-four walnut-sized balls. Place six in a circle on
a microwave baking tray. Press on each ball with a fork to flatten slightly.

■

MICROWAVE on MEDIUM for $3\frac{1}{2}$ minutes. Leave to stand for 5 minutes,
then transfer to a wire rack to cool. Repeat with the remaining balls.

Fresh Fruit Tartlets (page 55)

• CHOCOLATE, NUT AND RAISIN COOKIES •

This recipe makes two kinds of cookies, one flavoured with chocolate drops and nuts and the other with orange rind and raisins. If preferred, don't divide the mixture into two and add the chocolate drops, nuts, orange rind and raisins to all of the mixture to make multi-flavoured biscuits.

MAKES 24

100 g (4 oz) softened butter or soft tub margarine
100 g (4 oz) light soft brown sugar
1 egg
30 ml (2 tbsp) milk
10 ml (2 level tsp) baking powder
5 ml (1 tsp) vanilla flavouring
pinch of salt

350 g (12 oz) plain flour
50 g (2 oz) cooking chocolate drops
25 g (1 oz) nuts, such as almonds or walnuts, finely chopped
50 g (2 oz) raisins
10 ml (2 level tsp) finely grated orange rind

■

PUT the butter or margarine, sugar, egg and milk into a large bowl and beat until smooth. Add the baking powder, vanilla flavouring, salt and flour and knead until smooth.

■

CUT the dough in half. Knead the chocolate drops and nuts into one half, and the raisins and orange rind into the other half.

■

SHAPE the dough into twenty-four walnut-sized balls. Place eight balls in a circle on a microwave baking tray. Press on each ball of dough with a fork to flatten slightly.

■

MICROWAVE on MEDIUM for 3½ minutes. Cool for a few minutes, then carefully transfer to a wire rack to cool. Repeat with the remaining balls.

· APRICOT SLICES ·

The no-need-to-soak variety of dried apricots are best for this recipe. The slices can also be made with dried dates or figs.

MAKES 12

275 g (10 oz) no-soak dried apricots, finely chopped
100 g (4 oz) plain flour

100 g (4 oz) butter or margarine
100 g (4 oz) light soft brown sugar
100 g (4 oz) porridge oats

■

PUT the apricots and 150 ml ($\frac{1}{4}$ pint) water into a bowl and microwave on HIGH for 5 minutes. Cool slightly, then purée in a blender or food processor.

■

PUT the flour into a bowl and rub in the butter or margarine until the mixture resembles fine breadcrumbs. Stir in the sugar and oats.

■

PRESS half of the mixture into the base of a shallow 23 cm (9 inch) square dish. Stand on a roasting rack and microwave on HIGH for 2 minutes until the mixture bubbles all over.

■

SPOON the apricot purée evenly over the cooked oats and sprinkle with the remaining oat mixture. Microwave on HIGH for 4 minutes. Mark into 12 slices while warm and leave to cool in the dish. When cold, turn out and serve cut into slices.

· CARAMEL SHORTBREAD ·

Take care when making the filling for these shortbread bars – because of its high sugar content, the mixture and the bowl will get very hot.

MAKES 16 BARS

175 g (6 oz) plain flour
50 g (2 oz) caster sugar
175 g (6 oz) butter or margarine
50 g (2 oz) light soft brown sugar

400 g (14 oz) can condensed milk
100 g (4 oz) plain chocolate, broken into small pieces

■

PUT the flour and caster sugar into a bowl and rub in 100 g (4 oz) of the butter or margarine until the mixture resembles fine breadcrumbs. Press the mixture evenly into the base of a shallow 23 cm (9 inch) square dish.

■

MICROWAVE on HIGH for 2–3 minutes until the mixture puffs slightly all over and feels firm to the touch. Press lightly back into shape and leave to cool in the dish.

■

WHEN the shortbread is cold, put the remaining butter, sugar and condensed milk into a large ovenproof bowl. Microwave on HIGH for 5–6 minutes until boiling and a creamy fudge colour, stirring occasionally. Use a large bowl as the mixture bubbles up and can boil over.

■

POUR the caramel over the shortbread and spread evenly. Leave to cool.

■

WHEN the caramel is cold, put the chocolate into a bowl. Microwave on LOW for 4–5 minutes or until melted, then spread on top of the caramel. Leave to set in the refrigerator, then cut into sixteen bars.

▪ APPLE AND OAT SLICES ▪

If you have not got a microwave dish with a loose bottom,
cook these slices in a china flan dish and serve straight from
the dish.

MAKES 8 TO 10

100 g (4 oz) butter or margarine
50 g (2 oz) light soft brown sugar
30 ml (2 tbsp) clear honey
225 g (8 oz) porridge oats

350 g (12 oz) cooking apples, peeled,
cored and thinly sliced
5 ml (1 level tsp) ground cinnamon

▪

GREASE a shallow 20.5 cm (8 inch) round dish, preferably with a loose
bottom. Put the butter or margarine, sugar and the honey into a bowl and
microwave on HIGH for 1 minute until melted.

▪

ADD the porridge oats and stir until coated in the melted mixture.

▪

SPOON half of the oat mixture into the dish and spread evenly over the base.
Arrange the apples over the top and sprinkle with the cinnamon. Sprinkle
the remaining oat mixture over the apples and gently press down.

▪

STAND on a roasting rack and microwave on HIGH for 12–15 minutes until
the mixture feels just firm all over. Mark into wedges while warm, then
leave to cool in the dish.

▪ TRADITIONAL SHORTBREAD ▪

Shortbread is traditionally very pale, so it is well suited to
cooking in the microwave. The ground rice helps to give a
crunchy texture.

MAKES 8 PIECES

100g (4 oz) plain flour
50 g (2 oz) ground rice
100 g (4 oz) butter

50 g (2 oz) caster sugar
caster sugar, for dredging

▪

GREASE a shallow 20.5 cm (8 inch) round loose-bottomed dish.

▪

PUT the flour and ground rice into a bowl and rub in the butter until the
mixture resembles fine breadcrumbs. Stir in the sugar and knead together to
form a firm dough.

▪

PRESS the mixture into the dish and level the surface. Prick all over with a
fork, then microwave on HIGH for 5 minutes or until the surface of the
shortbread looks dry.

▪

COOL slightly, then mark into eight wedges. When the shortbread is
completely cool, turn out and sprinkle generously with caster sugar.

▪ Scottish Oatcakes ▪

Nobody will guess that you have cooked these light crisp
oatcakes in the microwave.

Makes 18

15 g (½ oz) lard
100 g (4 oz) fine oatmeal
pinch of salt

pinch of bicarbonate of soda
oatmeal, for rolling

▪

Put 150 ml (¼ pint) water and the lard in a jug and microwave on HIGH for
2 minutes.

▪

Put the oatmeal, salt and bicarbonate of soda into a bowl and add enough
of the hot water and lard mixture to bind into a firm dough.

▪

Roll out the dough on a work surface, sprinkled with oatmeal, to a
thickness of 0.3 cm (⅛ inch).

▪

Using a 6.5 cm (2½ inch) round cutter, cut out eighteen rounds,
re-rolling as necessary.

▪

Place six rounds in a circle on a microwave baking tray and microwave on
HIGH for 1½ minutes. Turn the oatcakes over and microwave on HIGH for
a further 2 minutes. Transfer to a wire rack to cool. Repeat with the
remaining rounds. Serve with cheese.

ICINGS AND DECORATIONS

For easy reference, a collection of icings and decorations is included here. Many cakes in the book can be varied with just a change of icing.

· GLACÉ ICING ·

MAKES ABOUT 100 G (4 OZ)

The quantities given make sufficient to cover the top of an 18 cm (7 inch) cake or up to eighteen small cakes. To cover the top of a 20.5 cm (8 inch) cake, increase the quantities to 175 g (6 oz) icing sugar and 30 ml (2 tbsp) warm water. This will give a 175 g (6 oz) quantity of icing.

Glacé icing can be used to coat a cake or if made a little stiffer, it can be piped. To make a piping bag, fold a 25.5 cm (10 inch) square of greaseproof paper diagonally in half, then bring the points round together to form a cone. Fold the points inwards to secure them. Spoon in the icing; do not fill more than half-full. Fold the top flap down, enclosing the front edge, until the bag is sealed and quite firm. Snip off the tip.

100 g (4 oz) icing sugar | *15–30 ml (1–2 tbsp) warm water*

■

Sift the icing sugar into a bowl. If you wish, add a few drops of any flavouring and gradually add the warm water. The icing should be thick enough to coat the back of a spoon. If necessary add more water or sugar to adjust the consistency. Add colouring, if liked, and use at once.

VARIATIONS

Orange Replace the water with 15 ml (1 tbsp) strained orange juice.

Lemon Replace the water with 15 ml (1 tbsp) strained lemon juice.

Chocolate Dissolve 10 ml (2 level tsp) cocoa powder in a little hot water and use instead of the same amount of measured water.

Coffee Flavour with 5 ml (1 tsp) coffee essence or dissolve 10 ml (2 level tsp) instant coffee granules in a little hot water and use instead of the same amount of measured water.

Mocha Dissolve 5 ml (1 level tsp) cocoa powder and 10 ml (2 level tsp) instant coffee granules in a little hot water and use instead of the same amount of measured water.

Liqueur Replace 10–15 ml (2–3 tsp) of the measured water with the same amount of any liqueur.

▪ BUTTER CREAM ▪

MAKES 250 G (9 OZ)

The quantities given make sufficient to coat the sides of an 18 cm (7 inch) cake, or give a topping and a filling. If you wish to coat both the sides and give a topping or filling, increase the amounts of butter and sugar to 100 g (4 oz) and 225 g (8 oz) respectively. This will make a 350 g (12 oz) quantity.

75 g (3 oz) butter
175 g (6 oz) icing sugar
a few drops of vanilla flavouring

15–30 ml (1–2 tbsp) milk or warm water

■

CREAM the butter until soft and gradually sift and beat in the sugar, adding a few drops of vanilla flavouring and the milk or water.

VARIATIONS

Orange or lemon Replace the vanilla flavouring with a little finely grated orange or lemon rind. Add a little juice from the fruit, beating well to avoid curdling the mixture.

Walnut Add 30 ml (2 level tbsp) finely chopped walnuts and mix well.

Almond Add 30 ml (2 level tbsp) finely chopped toasted almonds and mix well.

Coffee Replace the vanilla flavouring with 10 ml (2 level tsp) instant coffee granules blended with some of the liquid, or replace 15 ml (1 tbsp) of the liquid with the same amount of coffee essence.

Chocolate Replace 15 ml (1 tbsp) of the liquid with 25–40 g (1–1½ oz) chocolate, melted, or dissolve 15 ml (1 level tbsp) cocoa powder in a little hot water and cool before adding to the mixture.

Mocha Dissolve 5 ml (1 level tsp) cocoa powder and 10 ml (2 level tsp) instant coffee granules in a little warm water taken from the measured amount. Cool before adding to the mixture.

· CONTINENTAL BUTTER CREAM ·

MAKES ABOUT 300 ML (½ PINT)

The quantities given make sufficient to coat the top and sides of a 20.5 cm (8 inch) cake.

15 ml (1 level tbsp) cornflour
40 g (1½ oz) caster sugar
150 ml (¼ pint) milk

1 egg yolk
75 g (3 oz) icing sugar
175 g (6 oz) butter, softened

■

BLEND the cornflour, sugar and a little of the milk together. Put the remaining milk into a medium bowl and microwave on HIGH for 1–1½ minutes or until just boiling. Pour on to the cornflour mixture and stir well. Microwave on HIGH for 1–1½ minutes until thickened, stirring frequently.

■

COOL slightly, then beat in the egg yolk and microwave on HIGH for 1 minute, stirring frequently. Cover with a piece of greaseproof paper and leave until cold.

■

SIFT the icing sugar into a bowl, then add the butter and beat together. Fold in the cold custard and use as required.

· SEVEN-MINUTE FROSTING ·

MAKES ABOUT 175 G (6 OZ)

The quantities given make sufficient frosting to cover an 18 cm (7 inch) cake. To cover the top and sides of a three or four layer cake, double the quantities.

1 egg white
175 g (6 oz) caster sugar

pinch of salt
pinch of cream of tartar

■

PUT all the ingredients into a bowl with 30 ml (2 tbsp) water and whisk lightly. Place the bowl over a pan of hot water and heat, whisking continuously, until the mixture thickens sufficiently to stand in peaks. This will take about 7 minutes depending on the whisk used and the heat of the water.

■

POUR the frosting over the top of the cake, spread with a palette knife and mark into swirls.

VARIATIONS

Orange Beat in a few drops of orange essence and a little orange food colouring before the mixture thickens.

Lemon Beat in a little lemon juice before the mixture thickens.

Caramel Substitute demerara sugar for the white sugar, following the same method as above.

Coffee Beat in 5 ml (1 tsp) coffee essence before the mixture thickens.

· COFFEE FUDGE FROSTING ·

MAKES ABOUT 400 G (14 OZ)

The quantities given will cover a 20.5 cm (8 inch) cake

50 g (2 oz) butter or margarine
100 g (4 oz) light soft brown sugar
45 ml (3 tbsp) coffee essence

30 ml (2 tbsp) single cream or milk
200 g (7 oz) icing sugar

PUT the butter or margarine, brown sugar, coffee essence and cream into a large bowl and microwave on HIGH for 1½–2 minutes until the butter or margarine has melted and the sugar dissolved, stirring frequently. Microwave on HIGH for 3 minutes, without stirring.

GRADUALLY sift in the icing sugar and beat with a wooden spoon until smooth, then continue to beat for 2 minutes until the icing is thick enough to spread. Use immediately, spreading with a wet palette knife.

VARIATION
Chocolate Omit the coffee essence and add 75 g (3 oz) plain chocolate, broken into small pieces, in step 1.

· APRICOT GLAZE ·

MAKES 150 ML (¼ PINT)

This quantity of glaze makes sufficient to glaze about eight 9 cm (3½ inch) fruit tarts or two 20.5 cm (8 inch) fruit cakes. To make a smaller quantity halve the ingredients and microwave on HIGH for 30 seconds–1 minute until boiling, then continue as below.
This glaze may be reheated on HIGH for 1 minute if necessary.

75 ml (5 level tbsp) apricot jam

PUT the jam into a small bowl and add 30 ml (2 tbsp) water. Microwave on HIGH for 1–1½ minutes until boiling, stirring occasionally. Sieve and use while still warm as required.

▪ CRÈME PÂTISSIÈRE (CONFECTIONER'S CUSTARD) ▪

MAKES 300 ML ($\frac{1}{2}$ PINT)

Makes sufficient to fill an 18 cm (7 inch) flan case.

2 eggs
50 g (2 oz) caster sugar
30 ml (2 level tbsp) plain flour

30 ml (2 level tbsp) cornflour
300 ml ($\frac{1}{2}$ pint) milk
few drops of vanilla flavouring

▪

PUT the eggs and sugar into a large bowl and whisk with an electric whisk until pale and creamy and the mixture leaves a trail when the whisk is lifted. Sift in the flour and cornflour, then beat well together.

▪

PUT the milk into a bowl and microwave on HIGH for 2–2$\frac{1}{2}$ minutes until just boiling. Gradually pour on to the egg mixture, stirring all the time. Add the vanilla flavouring.

▪

MICROWAVE on HIGH for 1$\frac{1}{2}$–2 minutes until very thick, stirring frequently. Cover and allow to cool before using as required.

▪ CHOCOLATE DECORATIONS ▪

Chocolate caraque Break 100 g (4 oz) chocolate into pieces, put into a bowl and microwave on LOW for 5–6 minutes until the chocolate has melted, stirring occasionally. Pour it in a thin layer on to a marble slab and leave to set until it no longer sticks to the hand when touched. Holding a large knife with both hands, push the blade across the surface of the chocolate to roll pieces off in long curls.

Chocolate curls Using a potato peeler, 'peel' thin layers straight from the block of chocolate. It is best if the chocolate is at room temperature and not hard.

Chocolate circles Make a sheet of chocolate as above and stamp out circles using a small round cutter.

Chocolate triangles Make a sheet of chocolate as above and cut it into six to eight triangles.

Chocolate squares Make a sheet of chocolate as above and cut into 2.5 cm (1 inch) squares.

▪ QUICK CAKE DECORATIONS ▪

Keep a selection of the following and you will never be without an instant finish for your cakes. For even more ideas, look round sweet shops, confectionery counters or large department stores, grocers and supermarkets.

Nuts Shelled walnuts, pecans, hazelnuts, pistachios, and almonds (have a selection of types).

Crystallised violets and roses Buy in small quantities and keep in a dark place or jar to avoid bleaching.

Angelica Look for a really good colour and not too much sugar. To remove sugar, soak briefly in hot water, then drain and dry well.

Chocolate and coloured vermicelli Buy in fairly small amounts, unless a favourite recipe needs a larger quantity for, say, coating the sides of a cake. Vermicelli stales and becomes speckled.

Silver dragées (balls) Keep in a dry place. Use tweezers for handling, as the colour can come off and they are difficult to grip. Dragées also come in a variety of other colours.

Hundreds and thousands Popular with children and very useful as a quick decoration.

Glacé and candied fruits Cherries, ginger and pineapple are the most useful. Will go sugary if kept too long.

Sugar coffee beans Found in sweet shops, these are ideal for coffee cakes and gâteaux.

Chocolate Choose plain eating chocolate for chopping and grating. Chocolate flavoured cake covering is useful for scrolls and curls and also for melting, but the flavour is not so good. Crumbled chocolate flake is a useful last-minute decoration.

THAWING CHART FOR BAKED GOODS AND PASTRY
DOUGH

To absorb the moisture of thawing cakes, breads and pastry, place them on absorbent kitchen paper (remove as soon as thawed to prevent sticking). For greater crispness, place baked goods and the paper on a microwave rack to allow the air to circulate underneath.

Type	Quantity	Approximate time on LOW setting	Special instructions
BREAD			
Loaf, whole Loaf, whole	1 large 1 small	6–8 minutes 4–6 minutes	*Uncover* and place on absorbent kitchen paper. *Turn* over during thawing. *Stand* for 5–15 minutes.
Loaf, sliced Loaf, sliced	1 large 1 small	6–8 minutes 4–6 minutes	*Thaw* in original wrapper but remove any metal tags. *Stand* for 10–15 minutes.
Slice of bread	25 g (1 oz)	10–15 seconds	*Place* on absorbent kitchen paper. *Time* carefully. *Stand* for 1–2 minutes.
Bread rolls, tea-cakes, scones, crumpets etc.	2 4	15–20 seconds 25–35 seconds	*Place* on absorbent kitchen paper. *Time* carefully. *Stand* for 2–3 minutes.

Cakes	2 small	30–60 seconds	*Place* on absorbent kitchen
	4 small	1–1½ minutes	paper.
			Stand for 5 minutes.
Sponge cake	450 g (1 lb)	1–1½ minutes	*Place* on absorbent kitchen paper.
			Test and turn after 1 minute.
			Stand for 5 minutes.
Jam doughnuts	2	45–60 seconds	*Place* on absorbent kitchen
	4	45–90 seconds	paper.
			Stand for 5 minutes.
Cream doughnuts	2	45–60 seconds	*Place* on absorbent kitchen paper.
	4	1¼–1¾ minutes	*Check* after half the thawing time.
			Stand for 10 minutes.
Cream éclairs	2	45 seconds	*Stand* for 5–10 minutes.
	4	1–1½ minutes	*Stand* for 15–20 minutes.
Choux buns	4 small	1–1½ minutes	*Stand* for 20–30 minutes.
PASTRY			
Shortcrust and puff	227 g (8 oz) packet	1 minute	*Stand* for 20 minutes.
	397 g (14 oz) packet	2 minutes	*Stand* for 20–30 minutes.

Index